To my dear Tom!

THE Private DICK DIARIES

Humorous and authentic anecdotes of

REAL LIFE PRIVATE INVESTIGATORS

Volume 2

RULES OF CRIMINAL CASES

Welcome to THE PRIVATE DICK DIARIES.

Our world is becoming more and more pessimistic, which makes it harder and harder to find things to laugh at.

This series is our way of giving you somewhere humorous to escape to, if only temporarily.

The Private Dick Diaries is a series of books about our "Rules" of investigating; things to do, and in some cases, things not to do.

Each story is based on real life cases of real life Private Investigators, and sadly enough the perpetrators are true too. No names are given, and times, places and items are slightly altered. This is to protect the innocent, the guilty and the idiots (the latter two usually being the same).

Enjoy the second book in the series, "Rules of Criminal Cases". We think you'll find as much humor and suspense in reading them as we did in solving them!

If you haven't already done so, be certain to check out Book #1, Rules of Repo.

Next in line is Book #3, Rules of Missing Persons.

TABLE OF CONTENTS

INTRO TO US

Hi, I'm Erin Jenkins, the one with his name on the cover. Thought I'd give you a little insight into the company, the staff, and how we all arrived where we are today.

First, a little explanation about the title of this book is in order. The "Dick" in the title refers to "Dick Tracy." He was a comic strip character created in 1931. Dick was formerly a commercial diver and served as a Lieutenant for Naval Intelligence, before tragedy struck and forever changed his life. He soon found himself a new career as a Police Detective. Dick was incorruptible, honest, and had an unswerving sense of justice. He used all the latest technology to find the truth and see justice served. Are you starting to get the picture? What were you thinking when you saw the title? If you didn't think of Dick Tracy – shame on you... ☺

I've had various careers in my life and I'm not at all surprised that I ended up being a Private Investigator, considering I started doing it when I was just a kid. I can remember being in the seventh grade; I raced BMX bikes and when my buddy's bike went missing I was convinced I knew who stole it. I did a little looking around, and talked to a few people, and all the information pointed toward the school's main thief and drug addict. I set up a sting and told him that I was looking to buy a bike, and proceeded to describe the exact model of my buddy's bike. He naturally had one, so we met and I busted him, literally. He wanted the cash and when I refused we went to the fists. Riding back on my pal's bike I knew I was on to something.

My experience came from three significant and totally opposite educators: the School of Hard Knocks, the military, and most importantly, my grandfather. He was the most influential person in my life. From a very early age I spent a lot of time with him; sometimes weeks and months at a time. I spent every summer and fall working and hunting with him. He was a brilliant man; he could design, build, repair or fix anything, and I mean anything.

He taught me how to think, how to solve problems and how to be creative. Thinking outside the box was the norm. I learned to never be afraid and try new ways to get from point A to point B because, even if I failed, I would learn something in the process. We had a very close relationship and to this day I make a lot of decisions based on advice he gave to me years ago. Why he picked me to invest his time and energy into I'm not sure, but I'm grateful each and every day that he did. It also taught me the kind of man I wanted to be – honest, fair, trustworthy, and dependable. I grew up logging, farming and building, and the greatest gift my grandfather gave me was confidence in my thinking and decision making ability.

I spent six years in the military as an Air Force cop. I worked nuclear missile security, base law enforcement, and the last two and a half years I was crew chief in the World's Largest Armory. I was a top-cop known for a no-nonsense work ethic, and because of this I was afforded a lot of specialized training. I have put this training into good use day in and day out as an investigator. My staff and friends call me the human lie detector; thank you USAF and the School of Hard Knocks. This has been critical to my work as a private investigator and has proven most valuable as a parent, especially as my kids enter their teen years.

Before my enlistment in the military was up, I was scouted for various other positions with the US Border Patrol, the Secret Service, the Department of Energy and the US Marshal's Office. All would have been extremely intriguing if it wouldn't have been for one very important thing; my wife and I wanted to raise a family and we weren't going to do so in a big city or a remote border town. These places are where all of these opportunities would have likely landed us.

Therefore, I took a different road, back to the logging industry in one of the USA's most beautiful and bountiful states: Idaho.

I worked hard and did very well. Then, on October 17, 1994, tragedy struck my life. From that point on my priorities started to change, and my work was starting to take away from one of my main priorities, my family.

So, I started doing some PI work part-time in 1997 and worked a few cases for a local attorney. I did the investigating at night and logged during the day.

I continued this for a few years, and with referrals from satisfied clients I built up my presence as an investigator. When I knew I could support my family, I sold the logging equipment and became a full-time private investigator.

To quote my grandfather, "work smart, work hard and don't quit until you have it right." I live this each and every day in both my personal and professional life, and our business continues to grow every year.

WHO WE ARE & WHY WE DO WHAT WE DO

Confidential Investigations is located in Hayden, Idaho. It's the perfect place to raise a healthy family. There are four definite seasons with endless outdoor activities keeping everyone busy and pleased.

I've often been asked why I became a PI and the bottom line, other than the flexibility to be there for my wife and kids, is that I'm out for justice. I wanted to use the skills I've developed over the years and put them to good use. I wanted to do something that would better the community where my family and friends live. Most importantly, I had to be able to do this without compromising my values. Confidential Investigations was built on this premise and we're known for doing things legally and morally. So, in developing the business, this is also what I expect from my employees. We dig up the truth and give it to our clients, regardless of what it is. If it helps, great; if not, it is what it is.

Kaleb

Kaleb looks absolutely nothing like what you'd think he would after talking to him on the phone. From his voice and volume you might picture a small-framed, meek, mild-mannered man. Kaleb is grand in all senses of the word and small is never used when describing anything about him.

Kaleb was working for a bail bond company and came into our office week after week attempting to convince us that we needed to hire him. I was impressed by his size but wasn't convinced of his intelligence. Big is nice, but in this business brains are stronger. No matter what I thought, he was persistent, enough so we decided to give him a try part-time. He started out serving papers and subpoenas and did great. Next we put him on surveillance and this is where I was gladly proven wrong.

He is patient, meticulous, and his ingenuity continually impresses all of us. He consistently gets the video footage and the information we need to succeed. He is now my right-hand man! Kaleb works everything from serves to major cases. His off-time is spent camping and raising his baby boy and girl. Those high school boys have no idea what they're up against when they start coming around knocking on her front door. Luckily for Kaleb that's still a few years off.

Sully

Sully was destined to be a part of Confidential Investigations. He is a retired 25-year-plus veteran homicide detective from California who is a cop at heart, and just wasn't ready to leave the business.

He moved to Idaho and headed up a local security company. After realizing the immoral and unethical nature of the company's owner, he left in order to not compromise his own beliefs and values. Upon this decision, he simply walked through the front door of my company and asked if we had work. We didn't at the time but I knew from our first meeting this was an individual I wanted to get to know better. We sat down for a pseudo job interview and I was immediately impressed.

Upon first appearance, Sully is humble and unassuming; it isn't until he speaks that you realize the depth of knowledge and experience he has in the field of major crimes. He is an expert in this field, as well as a specialist in crime scene preservation.

I brought him on as a consultant with a major murder case we were working on, and after more than proving his worth decided to take him on. As our business grew so did our need for his expertise.

We share the same demeanor and, on more than one occasion, have finished one another's thoughts and sentences. Being a military man, I never miss an opportunity to throw cops and donut jabs his way, to which he always has a clever response.

He is not only a qualified detective, but an upstanding and ethical human being; we are blessed to have him on board.

Beth

Beth is a retired general crimes and drug enforcement detective. Her nickname from her former co-workers is "Shorty" and the name is very fitting. The fitting part is in relation to her size, not her brain. I first met her many years ago when she was covering drug enforcement cases. I had an informant of mine who had some info that was in need of a "home". I made a call and talked with Beth and we hooked her up with a felony arrest. From that point on we found a home for many other pieces of homeless information with her. I just hate for anything to be homeless! After several years of her taking in our homeless, she retired and came to work with us. Beth loves to dig into a case and is not afraid to upset the apple cart. You just have to love that! It's also very nice to have a female perspective to bounce things off of around the office. When Beth first came on board with us and started working cases, I had to laugh at all the attorneys who were taken back by the fact she was working for us now. I would get comments like "You have got to be kidding me!"; "Thank God I don't have to go up against her anymore!" and "I can have her on my side??? AWESOME!!" Unlike what I say to Sully, I don't beat her up with donut jokes, but I do from time to time pretend I can't see her unless I'm looking at the ground! She is awesome to work with!

INTRO TO CRIMINAL CASES

Wiki definition: "If a person violates ANY statute or law passed by the state legislature which has been declared a crime, and to which a penalty for that crime has been attached, they become involved in a CRIMINAL CASE."

That definition can seem as clear as mud so let me help make it less ambiguous. A criminal case is one that results in a *charge* being filed. Charges can be a *misdemeanor*, a lesser crime with smaller consequences; or a *felony*, which is a much more serious crime and comes with a much more severe punishment. Felony convictions are those that serve one or more years in a prison, anything under that is a misdemeanor. Misdemeanors can also serve jail time. Both types of charges can have financial repercussions, as determined by the courts.

To make things a little more confusing, each state has its own set of rules when determining if the charge is a misdemeanor or felony, per its specific laws.

The crime determines the fine; now a standard DUI would more than likely be a misdemeanor, but if the drunk driver was in an accident which resulted in a death then they would have a felony on their hands.

The Mac-daddy's of the felonies, of course, are murder, rape, etc; these are the ones that can carry the death penalty. Then you have to take into consideration the degrees of each charge; 1st degree will serve more than, let's say, a 3rd degree crime. In Idaho, murder is the only felony that holds a penalty of death.

It's all quite intimidating as far as pin-pointing a definite definition since there are a ton of "what-ifs" needing to be taken into account. This may explain why our legal system takes so terribly long to actually complete a case, sometimes even years. So criminal can apply to a wide gamut of crimes.

Confidential Investigations is one of the only PI firms in the area actually *qualified* to investigate a death penalty case. Qualification is granted by the courts and is based on a high level of experience. We supply the attorney working the case with resumes on our investigators and he will have the court determine if we are qualified to investigate. Naturally, our firm is licensed, but we have only two investigators able to investigate these death penalty cases – me, and Sully.

We can be hired by numerous different sources; a private party (whether that's a business, an individual or a corporation), a private attorney, the prosecutor, or the public defender. In some instances we can investigate on behalf of a client before he/she actually files criminal charges. One such case comes to mind:

We were hired by a rather lucrative and large corporation who thought their bookkeeper might have been skimming off of them. If we found any proof then they could determine what steps they wanted to take from there. Well, we did in fact find evidence - to the tune of $60,000! I called her and told her to come down to the office so that we could talk. She wasn't exactly certain what she was coming in for, but she agreed, and showed up with her husband of nearly 30 years. She was not what I expected to see. She was in her late 50's, short with a bit of a weight issue, wearing a dowdy dress and her hair was in a bun sitting on the top of her head. A weaker man may have let that get to him, but a crime is a crime and I had a job to do. She sat down in the conference room next to her husband and I took my place on the other side, of course fully wired.

"You've been stealing from your company, right?"

She said nothing but as she dropped her head it became loud and clear. Her husband, on the other hand, obviously had no idea as his body language was completely opposite. He sat up straight, eyes and mouth open wide looking at me then at his wife, at me then his wife. I did feel for him as his life was about to change drastically and it had nothing to do with anything he did or even knew about.

"So how much would you say you've stolen?"

She finally looked up and obviously threw a number my way hoping to satisfy my question.

"About 5,000."

"Nope. Try $60,000."

She knew this was a much more accurate amount and when her husband quickly stood up out I was convinced he had no idea whatsoever; this was shocking news to him!

She managed to get her husband to calm down and attempted to explain to him her actions, all the while *not knowing it was being recorded.* She said it started when they were a few hundred dollars short on their monthly bills so she decided to take it from the company, with the intent of paying it back. When it seemed no one missed the money, she took a little more. From there it just became easier and easier. She ended her confession by trying to justify her actions, saying she hadn't gotten a raise in long while. It became like an addiction.

“Here’s the deal. You owe them 60 thousand dollars and you need to get it back to me by 5 o’clock today or I’ll have you in a set of handcuffs. Are you ready for that?”

She now realized the magnitude of her actions and even though tears fell on her cheeks, her husband made no motion to comfort her; I can’t say as I blame him. They ended up signing over *their house* to my client as the majority of the cash was gone, spent on who knows what.

The corporation’s attorney drew up the contract that held their house as collateral, and gave her 90 days to come up with the cash or lose their home. Technically it was a criminal case but we’ve learned from experience that if the client has any hope of getting their losses back, throwing the criminal in jail will not accomplish that.

If she went to jail she’d more than likely get a slap on the wrist and our client would have to sue her. It could take years, if ever, to see any payback. Not to mention the amount of cash it would take to battle this. So this really was the best way to deal with this particular criminal case. No charges filed.

The Judicial System

I'm going to take a moment to explain how our legal system works. I think as you read through the various cases you will gain a better understanding. Therefore, forgive me if you already are aware of this knowledge as I know you, our readers, are brilliant (we know that because you bought the book) but it never hurts to be thorough.

The structure I'm about to detail not only applies to the city, but also the county and the individual states which have similar organizations within them. It starts with the judges and the jury who preside over the court proceedings. They are the people who hear both sides of a case and then have the job of determining if the law applies in this case. This judge or jury is supposed to be impartial and base decisions on the information which both sides of the case have brought to their attention, as well as how the law applies. They're supposed to be.

Then we have the lawyers who represent both sides of the situation. A lawyer primarily falls into three categories; private practice, public defender or prosecutor.

Private practice lawyers consist of a variety of types; too many to list. *Some* examples of private practice lawyers are; criminal, corporate, civil, divorce, family, business, patent, bankruptcy, real estate, and the list goes on and on. Your individual situation dictates who you seek out.

We have all heard the following statement multiple times, and hopefully, it's only been on television: "You have the right to remain silent..., if you cannot afford a lawyer one will be provided to you." This lawyer is the public defender.

Many lawyers start their careers here, not exactly the top of the attorney food chain. They tend to be overworked and underpaid with numerous cases in the air at any given time. It's really a crap-shoot not knowing exactly the kind of representation you're going to get. So, don't get yourself in this position.

The prosecutor, or district attorney, is the one who does battle against the person who is being charged. His/her job is to present a case to the courts that proves the accused is, indeed, guilty.

The prosecutor is an elected position by the voting public, and is the only one who can file charges. There are also numerous deputy prosecutors who help the district attorney.

Here's an example of how this plays out:

- Someone breaks into your house and steals everything.
- You call the cops.
- They make an arrest *(wishful thinking)* and file the report with the prosecutor.
- Prosecutor presses charges.

  The accused hires a lawyer of his choice; on his nickel, or the public defender.
- The lawyers go head-to-head in court, and the judge or jury rules.

That's obviously the condensed version but it explains how we can end up on different sides of the law, still just trying to dig up the truth.

Now turn the page, get ready to laugh, and enjoy the "Rules"!

Rule #1:

NEVER TRY TO REASON WITH STUPIDITY

There are, of course, cases where criminal charges are inevitable. One of those situations actually happened as a result of a typical repo case we were hired to do. This assignment became known around the office as, "The B#*!h & Butthead" case. It started as only a potential misdemeanor, but due to their stupidity they managed to shift themselves into felons!

It started as a simple repo of a car, an older Cadillac that belonged to a drug dealer. *(If you haven't already, be sure to check out more stories in the first book of our series, Rules of Repo.)* Let me tell you, this car was the epitome of gangster style, a low rider in a matte black finish with obnoxiously shiny mag wheels! The only thing missing was the chain steering wheel and hanging fuzzy dice.

Kaleb and I did our usual pre-investigation work and found out the best time and place to repo the car. It worked out great. We had the car back at the office and we started bagging up the personal contents in case the repo-ees wanted their stuff back, which legally is theirs. It felt like a typical repo job, and we had the driver's wallet and his passenger's purse so we knew who they were. But what we found in the center console made it not so typical! We opened it up and found marijuana - not just a little bit but a lot! I called my contact, who just so happened to be a local drug enforcement undercover cop.

"You want something to do with this?" I asked. I also just happened to mention the name on the driver's license from the wallet.

"Hell YES, I'm on my way!"

Unfortunately, it's not as simple as arresting them because legally they weren't caught in possession. As a matter of fact, I was now technically in possession! So before any arrests were going to be made, they needed to confess that it was in fact their drugs.

While Kaleb and I waited for the officer we received a call from the passenger; the driver's girlfriend. I kept her on hold long enough to get my microphone hooked up to the phone.

"I want my stuff back," was her opening line.

"No problem. Sure, you can have it back."

"I'll be there in 10 minutes." was her next demand.

"No, you won't be here in 10 minutes. You can show up in 30 minutes, no sooner. And are you bringing your boyfriend with you?"

I could hear her slime of a boyfriend in the back ground and he was spewing profanities at me. I had had enough of their attitudes so I made certain to get her attention:

"You tell your friend, if he even thinks about coming to my office and making any kind of a stink I'll make both of your lives a living hell. You *do not* want to mess with us. Now tell him that!"

I waited as she repeated verbatim what I had told her and his silence told me exactly the type of coward we were dealing with.

"Hey, there's also a crap load of weed. Is it yours?" I waited, hoping she was stupid enough to take the bait. "I guess you can have that back because I don't even know what to do with it." A small untruth, as I knew exactly what to do with it.

"Yeah, yeah, it's mine."

Got her.

"And the pipes?"

"Yeah, they're mine too."

“Okay, we’ll see you when you get here in a half an hour, no sooner!”

My undercover pal showed up, and since he was getting ready to take off for the weekend, he was in flip flops and shorts. I wired him up and we decided it was best that our druggies think he’s one of my guys; what they don’t know won’t hurt them. Technically, he cannot search the car without a warrant, but I can. I was contracted to repossess the auto, so it legally is in my possession, which means I can go through it with a fine tooth comb. By law, if there happens to be any illegal items found I can turn it over to the authorities, which is exactly what I planned to do.

The undercover cop had his boss planted across the parking lot from us in an unmarked car with a video camera aimed right at the low-rider. I also adjusted our security camera to point in the same direction; we weren’t taking any chances on these two! We already had her and we were hoping he would follow her dim-witted lead. We had bagged up all of their possessions. The car was a mess; loaded with tons of garbage and, unfortunately, a kid’s car seat and multiple toys. The marijuana went right to the officer. The dim-wits had divided it and packaged it for resale which changes the intent from "personal use" to "distribution". This was no longer just a possession charge, this was intention to sell, both of which are felonies. We had to get the guy to admit it was his if we wanted the charges to stick.

They showed up on the half hour and I purposefully left them waiting in the reception area just to show them who was in charge. My undercover pal and I met them at the front desk and she came on as a b#*!h from hell. This didn't bother me as I knew where she was going, and she'd change her tune. Kaleb quickly joined us after he heard the ruckus; he wanted to be part of the action. The boyfriend was quiet, like I figured he would be, just strutting around all cool with his shaved head and tattooed arms. She was a large woman, wearing clothes that certainly weren't meant to be on her frame. She had a fair amount of tats herself, with bleach blonde straggly hair in a knot, on top of her head

"We've got your stuff all bagged up, but before we get to that there's something that I'm not really buying." I was directing my question towards the boyfriend.

"Your girlfriend said the weed belongs to her and for some reason that doesn't make sense to me." I was hoping this would be the opportunity to get him to fess up and we'd get both of them.

He didn't answer right away and after 30 seconds or so of "hos" and "hums" I interjected:

"No big deal, if you can't answer, we'll just get rid of it."

This was my bluff move considering the drugs were already logged into evidence at the police station.

"No, no it's mine, it's mine." Guess the thought of us trashing his stash didn't sit too well!

"You know I'm not buying that either. She said it was hers and now you say it's yours. So whose is it really? It's got to belong to both of you." The hook was thrown and hopefully they'd take the bait. Wait for it…wait for it.

"Well it's … it's really both of ours." He really didn't want to lose his drugs.

"Yeah, it's both of ours." She willingly chirped in. "That's why I said it was mine on the phone."

I looked over towards Kaleb and he was about to lose it. Kaleb even had to physically turn away to stop himself from laughing. These two idiots thought they were getting out of a lie, and I was letting them think so.

"Oh okay, so it's both of yours?" I asked again, just to make sure we had it on tape.

They both nodded and verbally confirmed their guilt, even though they didn't know it yet. All that was left to do was to lead them to the car and get their stuff.

We all just stood there and said nothing as he opened each bag one by one and obviously was searching for something in particular, something we knew he wasn't going to find. She came to me and said that there were some papers on the visor that she needed. I let her get them, but I stayed next to her boyfriend making certain two microphones were on him at all times. In hindsight I should have followed her, but at the time she wasn't our focus as we already had her confession.

"Where is it?" He asked, ironically looking at the undercover cop

"Where's what?" The detective does not like to be talked down to and it was obvious when he snapped back at the question.

"My weed!"

I looked over at my detective pal and could see that he was having trouble keeping a straight face, but he managed to pull it together. Without changing his facial expression a bit, he took a step closer to the punk and looked him directly in the eyes.

"I... burned...it."

Nothing else was said. He threw the rest of the belongings in the back of their van, barked at his girlfriend to get in and away they went. We waited until they were completely out of sight and could no longer contain ourselves. We busted out laughing!

So we had a repo that turned into a felony. That was a good day. But the story gets even funnier. Now, you may be wondering why the cops didn't just arrest them right then and there. To do it right, and be certain no loose ends are left dangling for some hungry lawyer to pull at, they had to get a warrant first. Seeing as how it was Friday they'd get one more free weekend and they had no idea of what was coming.

Kaleb went to move the car and called me on the phone. "She took the radio's faceplate."

"What!?" I was livid, that b#*!h (which is how this repo got its name) thought she could screw with me! This was nothing but a flip-off to us, and there was no way I was going to let it slide. I grabbed my cell and immediately dialed her number; no surprise that she didn't answer. The next call was to the boyfriend and he did pick up.

"Tell your girlfriend I want that faceplate back by 6 o'clock tonight!"

Now that there were some miles between us he obviously was feeling pretty tough. He let me know that he may tell her, or he may not, depending upon if he got around to it. That was *not* the right answer.

"Listen here, *punk*, you do not want to mess with me! It better be at my office or else you will regret it!"

"Are you threatening me?!"

"Am I threatening to beat the s#*! out of you? No. But if it's not back by 6 you will regret it, I promise that."

He hung up. I wanted *so* badly to be there Monday when the cop drove to his house and knocked on the door because you know as the idiot walked to the squad car with his hands cuffed behind his back, the only thought in his head was "should have brought the damn faceplate back".

So this case became a criminal one because, believe me, charges were indeed filed. Now sometimes we find ourselves on both sides of the legal spectrum. We may have been hired by the defense or by the prosecution, but regardless of who hired us our mission is always the same: to find the truth.

We often get the misinformed idiots who think we're trying to get the creeps off their charges and we're helping the ambulance chasing lawyers slip one over the courts. That simply isn't the case with us. We deal with the facts and only the facts. Sometimes it works out for our clients, and sometimes it doesn't, that's not my concern. All I care is that everyone has the truth, the undeniable facts. What they do with those after I uncover them is up to the attorneys and the judges. I never sway them one way or the other, that's not who I am and not how Confidential Investigations operates, period.

The good lawyers, and yes there are some, will take the facts and if they don't favor their client they will wisely advise a plea. But the bottom decision is up to the accused; if they take a "hell no" stand then the lawyer will go to battle. Unfortunately, or in some cases fortunately, their punishment is much worse than the pleas would have been. Again…not my concern. I deal with the truth only.

The Rule: If you smoke/deal weed and the best job you ever had was flagging traffic in construction zones, you are not as smart as we are!

A few months later I got a very bizarre phone call. It was a woman's voice and she wanted me to repo "her" car. It didn't start out being bizarre but as the woman continued telling me her story I could not believe my ears. I wasn't exactly sure at first, but as soon as she mentioned the car was an older Cadillac I knew who it was. She had blocked her number, but that wasn't an issue since I have this great program on my phone that unblocks them!

She was suing the client we repossessed the car for in the first place and wanted us to get it back for her. Hell no! I explained to her how not only was she not going to get the judgment, but that we would never breach our client's loyalty (especially with her).

She and her now ex-boyfriend made a deal with the cops. They agreed to give up the names of all their clientele in exchange for no jail time. Apparently, now that she was off the hook with the cops, she decided to go after the car she never paid for in the first place.

*I got off the phone and was laughing hard enough to attract Kaleb who came into my office to see what was up. He too thought that this was unbelievable; the things people, especially the stupid ones, think they can get away with! After this, we had to change her nickname from "b#!*h" to "delusional b#*!h".*

Rule #2:

ALWAYS UNDERESTIMATE THE INTELLIGENCE OF IDIOTS

It's easy to assume that most people who are guilty of crimes are stupid. Well, usually they are – and this case was no exception.

This case is about a break-in and vandalism, but before we can tell that story, we have to back up a bit to give you the bigger picture of what sent this stupid criminal into his downward spiral. Ironically, he wasn't even involved in the beginning; he volunteered his services at the end.

It started as a simple barroom quarrel that led to so much more. A man, let's call him David, was simply enjoying a game of pool with his best bud and his bud's wife. He was in his mid-thirties, not married, no kids, stood over 6 feet tall, with dark hair and a short beard. He would be considered skinny by most that saw him, maybe even using metaphors like string bean or bean pole. He had a good job, making enough to pay his bills and still had a little extra for a night out like this one to just hang with friends. He was a fairly decent guy who worked hard and stayed out of trouble.

So, there he was with his friend and his friend's wife shooting pool and having a few drinks. It was a Thursday evening so the bar wasn't packed but there were quite a few patrons there ready to start the weekend early. The bar-slash-pool hall was a familiar hang out for locals. It was a bit beat up and run down, but the low beer prices made up for the amenities and made it comfortable enough for most who frequented there. David and his pal had been playing for a while, not like they'd been hogging the table or anything like that, but it had been long enough for one particular customer who decided it was his turn to play. Let's call this one Ben.

So Ben and his pal wanted to play pool and they decided that they wanted David's table. If you know about pool halls, then you'll know that the appropriate etiquette is to *challenge* for the table. For most of us this would be a simple friendly competition where the loser gives up the table. Sometimes these people might even become friends, considering they share a common interest in pool. Well it could have been that if it weren't for Ben.

Ben was a known bully. He was the offspring of a rather famous actor from the eighties and he decided that alone should afford him the status of royalty and automatically put him on a pedestal above everyone else! Most of those who tagged around with him were also swinging off his daddy's purse strings and were nothing more than wannabes. They would do whatever Ben asked just to be blessed enough to be accepted into his precious circle of friends. He was a good-looking kid, tall with thick blonde hair, and in good shape; which made sense considering his day was filled with trips to the gym and then just hanging out wherever he wanted to with whomever he wanted to, and there were always plenty of willing leaches.

So Ben wanted to play, and instead of simply going over to David and his friends and requesting a game to see who keeps the table, he, in his arrogant way, walked over to the table and grabbed David's pack of cigarettes sitting on the edge. He pulled out a smoke and lit it all the while giving David the evil eye.

"What the hell are you doing?" David asked, not impressed at all.

David not only didn't know who Ben or his dad was, but he didn't care! Ben's behavior was unacceptable and David would never back down to a bully, especially a 20-something year-old punk. But Ben's arrogance made him blindly stupid. After a flurry of smack talk he made his challenge for the table clear. What he didn't stop to do first was to spend a few seconds actually watching David play, or he would have known that he was a much better pool player than himself. Regardless, the game was on and then the second and the third, all with the same results. Not just a win for David, but an ass-whooping for Ben.

With every loss, Ben became more and more agitated. He had nothing to back himself up with other than a smart mouth and idle threats; none of which David or his pal were buying. This only fed Ben's egotistical rage! Not knowing what else to do, Ben escalated his fury and became physically threatening to David, his pal, and his pal's wife. This dumb-ass was fueled with liquid courage and who knows what else. David did his best not to respond in the same way and refused to give in to Ben's depraved behavior.

The attempted scuffle caught the attention of the rest of the patrons. The tables were full and those that gathered were not the same as the typical weekend crowd, which explains why the response to the scuffle was somewhat ignored. The weekend warrior crowd would have rounded up the instant the first dirty look was thrown. Mind you, they would not have been there to break it up; it would have turned into tag team WWF match.

Fortunately, the bartender was well-versed in the body language of pre-fighting so he quickly got involved. The bartender was an ideal fit for this establishment. He was bald, big and neck-less. Tattoos suggested he may not be the tree you wanted to climb. As drunk as Ben and his buddy were, they knew it best to accept the bartender's option of leaving quietly versus having him throw both of them out on their butts. This was obviously not the bartender's first run-in with Ben, and he made it perfectly clear as he escorted them out that they were no longer welcome in this bar!

David and his friends had a nice laugh with the bartender, at Ben's expense, as he detailed multiple scuffles Ben had caused in the past. He was pleased that this would be the last time he'd have to jump in and save Ben from getting his butt kicked. After the stories and a complementary round of beers for what the bartender said was, "for having to endure the wrath of the trust fund baby," David and his friends got on with their evening and continued to shoot pool and BS. What they didn't imagine was that Ben would be patient and spiteful enough to wait all this time outside for David.

Two hours later, David decided to call it a night. He said goodbye to his friends outside the front door of the bar, and they went their separate ways. Unlike his friend, who left quickly, David had a bit of a walk to his truck. He didn't notice he was being watched until his friend had already driven away. It took him a few seconds more to realize exactly who was watching him and even though he outsized Ben, David was smart enough to know that a two-on-one situation isn't the best one to get backed into. He picked up his pace and ran to his vehicle.

David managed to make it into the driver's side, slam the door, and lock it just before Ben and his buddy reached him. Ben started off with multiple verbal threats while his sidekick hammered the windshield and passenger side window in an attempt to either get David to come out and "deal with it," according to Ben, or to get inside the truck themselves. Driving away wasn't an option, as they moved to the front of the truck and began beating on the hood. David had enough and resorted to the last option he felt was left; he reached under his seat with his right hand and pulled out a Taurus 9mm pistol. Ben didn't take the time to realize he was not in California anymore. In Idaho, a lot of us pack guns. It's easy to tell the non-native weapon carriers from the rest of us; they're the ones with the bumper stickers that read "Keep Honking…I'm Reloading". We Idahoans look at that as a bit puzzling considering that our big guns have matching big magazines so we don't have to waste time reloading. Not to mention we know how to shoot and our aim is excellent!

David cracked the window, drew their attention to what he was holding, and essentially told them to "back off if they knew what was good for them." Very "bad guy 101" verbiage but he eloquently got his point across. Ben and his pal slowly backed away from the front of David's truck and he quickly drove off. Should have been a drunken done deal, should have been.

Ben was not pleased this was the second time he had been put in his place and he was having none of it. He turned to his buddy and informed him that it was time to stop playing. Not certain if Ben was about to pull a gun of his own out of his pocket, his pal held his breath until he saw Ben was indeed reaching for something, a cell phone. Ironically, this turned out to be almost as deadly for David.

Using his best acting skills, which were no doubt handed down from his daddy's genes, Ben dialed 911. His dad had played a good cop in the eighties films. I wonder what happened to his apple. It rolled far away from the family tree, that's for sure! Ben's story was elaborate and really quite brilliant considering his level of anger and inebriation. His version started with the bar fight, instigated by David of course, and led to the parking lot where he said he was not only threatened by a gun but that two shots were fired at him. He was extremely cooperative giving the police a detailed description of not only David, but his truck, license plate, the time he left, the direction he went, and, of course, details about the gun. He also volunteered his services if they needed to ask more questions of him, politely leaving his address and cell phone number.

David was set up; set up in an extremely horrific way. The cops took only minutes to find him and upon seeing the red lights flashing behind him, David immediately feared losing his license but never imagined he could potentially lose his life. There he was. Just as Ben described and so was the gun. David was thrown up against the hood of his truck, handcuffed and thrown in the back seat of the police car like a common criminal, because that's what all the "evidence" pointed towards.

David's job was one he had been at for the last 12 years and, like most of our jobs, a felony never sits well with an employer. His job and his integrity in the community was being threatened, and it wasn't until the next morning when he was finally given the details of "victim Ben's" account that he knew how seriously in trouble he was. Evil minds are hard to fight especially since they believe they are entitled. They'll stop at nothing to get their way. In

Ben's mind he was made a fool of and no one was going to get away with it. David realized this as he found himself looking out from behind bars. He was going to need help to defeat this enemy. Ben was so proud of himself for his quick thinking and actions but David had so much more to lose. He was in a tough spot and things were not looking good for him.

David retained the services of an extremely qualified attorney who, in turn, was brilliant enough to hire us. Our mission was not going to be easy considering the only people who actually knew the truth was our client, plus Ben and his buddy, whom we were pretty certain would never snitch on his pal.

First, we started digging up any information we could find on Ben. The second item on the to-do list was to interview him and as many of his so-called friends that we could. Since it was a he said/he said situation, we needed to effectively discredit Ben's character and prove his complaint was false.

One advantage to being a licensed private eye is we have access to multiple websites that allow us to investigate details for our clients. In this case, Ben wasn't a stranger to the courts. He had numerous documented cases including drug dealing, multiple assaults and battery, and even mentions of some involvement with underage girls. Nothing major had ever stuck as good lawyers and money for his bail were always available. He received nothing more than a slap on the hand. His hand should have been blood raw from all the slaps! There were always witnesses but no one was rolling over on him. They knew going against Ben would be an extremely unwise choice.

Unfortunately being a POS (piece of #*^!) isn't enough to convict someone. Sad really, seeing how that would certainly benefit the world!

So, we had to turn our attention to Ben's entourage. Finding people to admit they are friends of his was easy; they wore the title like a badge of honor. Fortunately for us that badge was easily removed with a little push. We don't use threats, pressure, or bullying, merely influential persuasion. If I can get a few minutes with a person and engage in a little conversation, I can quickly read their personality and know exactly how to get to the real truth. That's the little push some of Ben's pals needed.

One interview led to two more, and when push came to shove they all admitted Ben wasn't the upstanding citizen he portrayed to the officers during his infamous 911 call. One interview we did with a gal provided us not only with valuable information for *our client*, it uncovered a whole *separate* tangent we morally *could not* overlook!

This side story from the gal's interview will give you a better idea of exactly what kind of individual we were dealing with. We'll call this girl Beth. Beth was barely 18 years old, even though she dressed, acted, and spoke much older. She volunteered pictures and texts from her cell phone that were sent to her by mistake from a guy we'll call "Keith". It was obvious they were meant to go to *Ben*, as the sender used Ben's name multiple times in the texts! We guessed Keith must have had fat thumbs and merely hit the name Beth, instead of Ben, from his contact list. Regardless, we had this incriminating evidence and needed it to go into the proper hands. Beth was visually relieved we were willing to take it off her hands. She commented that she had no idea what to do with them. We reassured her that we did.

These pictures were enough to turn any parent's stomach, especially those of us with daughters. Keith was not my priority, my client David was, but I was going to do everything in my power to get this slime put behind bars! The texts referred to his latest "conquests" and how great the "potion" worked. The pictures accompanying his words left nothing for the imagination and were beyond sickening. I felt enraged, and nauseous, trying to decide whether or not Ben lying to the cops should become secondary to this creep's crap! I wanted Keith's head on a platter and another part of his anatomy cut off! We had the pictures and texts recorded from Beth's phone, and before she got to her car I was on the phone with one of *the best* local sex-offender detectives around.

"Happy Birthday, Detective, I'm about to make you look good and all of us feel great...." Needless to say, Keith was in custody *that afternoon* and was quickly convicted. His sentence assured us parents of daughters many years of safety. Ironically, years later, the lawyer who was hired by Keith's family called me to see if I could help clear their "poor son's" name. (Keith, upon release, promptly got arrested again). The lawyer barely got their last name out before I told him I would not go anywhere near this case because it was a losing battle. He trusted me and wisely didn't take the case. Knowing Keith was behind bars and that we helped put him there left me with a good feeling inside. The fact that he was a small, scrawny molester who now has to fend for him-self in state prison makes me feel even better. Our streets and kids are just a bit safer without this slime.

Now we put our focus back on Ben. Friend after so-called friend came forward spewing garbage on Ben, enough to more than discredit his statement to the police against David. They may not have been so forthcoming if they knew that I was wired, but Idaho law states that only one of the two parties needs to be aware that they are being recorded. I knew, so we were good to go.

There was another interviewee who stood out more than the others, and he was particularly fun to deal with. He started off being very loyal to Ben and was arrogant in his own way. He was a self-proclaimed bi-sexual that spoke of Ben like he was an idol of some sort. It appeared to us that he may have had a bit of a man crush on Ben even though he knew Ben didn't swing that way (his words not mine). This interviewee had nothing but pleasantries to say about Ben, until I threw a subpoena in front of him and asked if he was up to lying in front of a judge. He recognized what that meant and quickly backtracked. He had a *complete* meltdown and spilled his guts! I'm not sure if he thought if he gave up Ben he'd be off the hook, which is silly considering *he wasn't being accused* of anything other than association. He spewed out stories about Ben dealing and using drugs; to fights Ben started; and even touched on his own involvement with the minors and their mutual pal

Keith. He obviously hadn't heard the ending to the Keith story, but regardless he verified everything we already knew about Ben. It was a nice addition to our case.

Seeing how dear Ben had been in multiple mishaps prior to this one, Daddy more than likely had a pretty swift lawyer of his own on retainer and ready for battle. In this case, Ben was the supposed *victim* so there was no need to call in his bulldog legal representative as this was up to a county prosecutor. David's attorney was sitting on a *gold mine* of testimonies and presented this prosecutor with the following option:

"If you decide to pursue these charges against my client…we will drag Ben to the ground and stomp the crap out of him. And it'll be for a lot more than a false 911 call. I suggest you have a little chat with him."

Not quite willing to raise the white flag just yet, the prosecutor decided to do his own interviews. We gladly gave him the list of names and contact numbers we had used. He was feeling a little hopeful, and smug, when these same people had a completely different take on their friend than what they had told us. This didn't surprise us a bit, because enough time had passed giving Ben plenty of opportunity to coach his acquaintances and tell them exactly what to say. The one thing he didn't know, however, was that all of the conversations we had with his "friends" had been recorded! When the prosecutor *attacked* David's attorney with his proverbial guns blaring, David's attorney countered with not only notarized copies of the transcripts, but recordings of the interviews as well! After reviewing all the material we had obtained, the prosecutor knew it was game-over. I would have loved to be in the room when he played the tapes for the liars, to see their jaws dropping on the conference table would have been priceless!

The charges, most of the charges, were dropped against David. There was the obvious driving-after –having-too-many-beers to contend with and David pled guilty to a DUI. Driving under the influence compared to driving while intoxicated carries a much lesser charge, and would not affect his long term record or his job. He did have a legal license to carry a concealed weapon, that wasn't a big deal. Authorities do frown upon flaunting it in public, so David was also charged with "exhibition of a weapon". Things worked out fairly well for our client. He had to contend with a few misdemeanors, but considering he was up for felonies he was glad to take what came his way.

The charges were reduced against David to what was right. He kept his job and is living his same life. Not sure if he still shoots pool or not, but my guess is he invested in a table of his own and invites his friends over to play at his house!

Chances are, Ben is back doing his thing too and there's even a bigger chance that he's still doing a lot of the same *wrong* things. I'm certain we'll hear his name again and when that time comes I'll be more than willing, once again, to do our part.

We were compensated for our job; the folders were filed away; and our job was done. We had no reason to think otherwise, even after the next morning, we still thought the same.

Okay, ready? This is where our original story starts; the one about the break-in and vandalism:

It was an early-winter, Monday morning. Fresh snow was on the ground and I was heading in to get a jump on the week. I saw the drifts in the parking lot and resigned to spending the morning shoveling. Before I got to my office door my cell phone rang. The neighboring business manager called and informed me of *the break-in.* I was willing to shovel snow, but I wasn't ready to shovel glass.

Our office is in a strip mall style building. The building is "L" shaped and we are smack dab in the middle. There is a double, glass-door entrance which puts you into a shared foyer. Upon entering the foyer there are two more single solid wood doors. Our office is to the right as you walk in, and another business's office is to the left. The glass door on the *right side* of the foyer was shattered and a broken wine bottle was resting on the foyer floor; comfortably out of the snow.

Without disturbing anything, wanting to make certain things were done by the book, the neighbors called the local authorities. I waited outside until they arrived and started taking pictures on my phone of not only the shattered door, but also the snow tracks around the building. Apparently our little night-stalker parked behind our building and came from the back door but decided to make a bigger impact by leaving his mark on the main entrance, literally. Our office has a fairly large picture window just outside the foyer doors; you actually walk past it to get to the main entrance. He decided to leave us a note, and using red spray paint he sprayed the words "BLOOD $$" in huge bold letters across the entire glass panel. He left a *less creative* message on the actual front door of our office. It was really uninspiring. Anyone could have come up with those two words and he didn't even bother to spell out the last word, just a lazy capital "U." There was also a handwritten note left, but we'll get into that a bit later.

I knew what the first question out of the officer's mouth would be, and I was already trying to come up with answers before he asked me "Who would want to do this to you?" Considering that we make a living out of exposing immoral, illegal and idiotic behaviors, it was hard to come up with just one suspect. Most of the people we piss off already know they are guilty; they just don't like being caught. The first choice that popped into my mind was a fairly recent case where we investigated a hunter after he shot a property owner. He was incarcerated thanks to us, but his little brother was on the loose and not happy. He easily moved to suspect number one. Unfortunately, well maybe fortunately, the officer recognized his name and told me that he caused a little grief himself that weekend and had spent the night in question "sleeping it off" behind bars.

The officer seemed discouraged, like maybe we had hit a dead end. I knew better so I looked up and pointed his attention to the ceiling. Owning a PI firm we have access to a lot of the cool "spy" gadgets. I would have thought most people would consider this but our guy didn't use too much of any thought process and we were about to find out exactly how little brain power he used. I couldn't wait to review the surveillance recording from our not-so-conspicuous cameras! We all gathered in the conference room to watch; with great anticipation of the possible highlights ahead. It started to feel like a mini-movie-premiere-viewing-party. I just wish we had time to get popcorn because this was hopefully going to be moment we all would remember forever.

The best picture I was hoping for was maybe a hand with a tattoo, or a side profile to work with. We were all gathered around the screen in the conference room as I started the review. The cameras are motion-activated and time-stamped, so I turned to Phil and asked him what time he left the night before. We started the review at that time.

5:07:13 The wine bottle crashes through the window as the camera picks up shards of glass flying against the wall.

5:07:25 A hand with a note comes through the broken opening.

5:07:29 Our suspect kicks out the remaining glass to make the opening bigger. "This is great!" I thought we might get a look at the top or side of his head! I was certain his face would be covered.

5:07:33 Here he comes; we see the right hiking boot, then the jean leg, then the shoulder of a sweatshirt, and a head. What? An *uncovered* head, NICE!

5:07:37 He paints his short, to the point, profanity on the door.

5:07:47 This is where it got priceless. He freezes and slowly moves his head to the right and looks up. We got him!

There he was, staring right at the camera lens with a wonderful "deer in the headlight," "oh crap," dumb look on his face! At this time, one of our investigators shouts out, "Smile Idiot, you're on candid camera!" We were laughing so hard I actually had to pause the recording! But we weren't done giggling just yet.

5:07:55 Not knowing what to do next, he reaches with his paint can up towards the lens and attempts to spray over it. Not only did the spray not reach the lens, but he gave us an even clearer picture of himself! Realizing this, he panicked.

5:08:03 He drops the can and bolts out of the glass the same way he came in less than a minute ago.

5:08:06 A note comes flying into the broken glass opening.

The note he left was handwritten on a scrap piece of white paper and in ordinary blue, ballpoint ink.

Eloquently written with a mix of random capitals and small letters, it read:

"IF YOU WILL CONVICT THE INNOCENT TO GET TO YOUR CLIENT'S WALLET YOU WILL GO TO HELL!!!"

That alone got a chuckle. The real kicker was, none of us knew who this kid was, let alone why he would have a bone to pick with us! But I knew how we could find out quickly. I first got the approval from the police, doing it by the book (remember), and they agreed I had a good idea.

Every citizen in the immediate area with a newspaper subscription woke up to HIS picture on the front page, that same stunned face we saw staring up at our camera with the caption, "Vandal caught on tape – Can you name him?" The calls started coming in to us and the police station. It was refreshing to see so many law-abiding citizens wanting to help, as well as an unusually large number of hopeful bitter ex-wives swearing it was their deadbeat ex-husbands. The same name started to pop up over and over.

The first time I saw his picture a faint déjà vu came over me and after I heard his name it all came back. He had changed since I last saw him; he cut his hair shorter, shaved and was wearing glasses. Thanks to the lady making the call, we not only had a name but we knew where he worked and now we had his motive.

It was Ben's boy crush from the interviews during David's case!

It had been months ago but obviously Ben was still annoyed with us. He somehow managed to get his *buddy* to fight his battle and attempt to defend his honor; as if he actually had some. The only thing I could think of was I hoped Ben was worth it because this dude was in very, very big trouble.

It was time to reintroduce myself to our vandal so I strapped on a wire and headed down to his work. The lady caller happened to be the receptionist at his place of employment and she kindly told us that he was, in fact, on duty right now. She also was very helpful and pointed him out to me when I arrived at their office. He was an employee of a local shop that repaired and sold used cars. Need I say more? Used car guys are a separate breed and you know what they say, "You know the only reason a used car salesman quit selling cars? He got fired."

Knowing full well who he was, I walked right up to him and asked, "Are you Darren?"

"Yes, I am. What can I do for you?" He asked quite nicely. I guess he had trouble remembering me.

"Nothing," was all I said as I grabbed my cell phone and started dialing.

"Can I help you?" He asked one more time.

"Nope, I'm just going to have your ass arrested."

Now he remembered me! I half expected him to bolt, so I was surprised by what he requested of me next.

"Not at work; please don't call the cops."

What in the hell made him think I owed him anything? But I was having fun so I thought I'd play along. He begged me "please, please not here, let's go outside and talk." Together we walked out to the parking lot where I asked if he did it, and he responded in kind with a full blown confession. He even volunteered how Ben convinced him to do this for him; nothing we could get on Ben, but it proved just how much of a follower he was. Our little chat lasted less than 5 minutes and I asked him to give me his driver's license. I took it from him, walked into the front office, went behind the desk, and made a photo copy like I worked there. No one tried to stop me! Word spread quickly about his newspaper debut so they just all watched in silence!

I was pretty much done with him and had more than I needed. I went to walk away and was validated that I had successfully scared the crap out of him because as I walked away, he stopped me to ask a ridiculous question:

"Should I get a lawyer?"

The first thought that popped into my head was, "Sure I know a few lawyers I can recommend." Unfortunately for him they were the *incompetents* of the trade. I refrained and responded with the only thing that came to mind:

"Don't bother; no one can save you now."

With that, I went to my car and made a call to the police on my drive back to my office. This incident happened on a Thursday and I managed to convince the officer in charge to let him be for today. I also told him to drop by my office in the morning for a cup of coffee and a laugh. I told him to conveniently show up at his work Friday, that way we'd be certain he'd have to spend the weekend in lock up. I'm sure Darren appreciated the time to think… He was arrested Friday at 8:00 a.m. for Burglary And Felony Malicious Injury To Property, and was handcuffed in front of his fellow employees.

During our chat he did mention an accomplice of sorts. He said a girl was with him but she stayed in the car while he broke in. I guess he thought it would lessen his punishment if he spread the guilt around! He also said he thought she got pretty scared and may have left town. She wasn't our concern but, being a father, I felt it was my obligation to help set her on the path of straight and narrow. I easily got her cell number and found out she did pack up and was staying in Seattle with a girlfriend. It was a good decision on her part and I did my part by scaring her into staying away from the likes of Ben and his "boyfriend". I hope it sticks. She seemed like a nice enough girl, just searching for somewhere to belong.

Local attorneys are familiar with us and the work we do and it's not like Darren could afford much so his case fell on the desk of the public defender. She was not only a new addition to the courts but a new addition to the industry. She wanted to prove herself as one of the "big boys" so she was pleased to have this opportunity. We were pleased for her too; well, let's just say we were pleased she had the case.

We did our part, and after gathering all the evidence it included copies of the surveillance video, the written note, pictures of the crime scene, as well as the recorded confession. We packaged it all nicely up and wrapped it with a bow for the detective. Needless to say, he was pleased too. We gave it to him and he, in turn shared it with the prosecutor who, in turn, gave it to the public defender, who wasn't as impressed by us.

We of course made ourselves available in case they needed us for any specific reason. The prosecutor didn't talk to us since our evidence spoke for itself, but I was glad to attend the sentencing hearing. I was there to hear the public defender's argument. Her statement was met with *complete* silence, then a few not-so-quiet snickers, one of them being mine. She opened with admittance that her client *was* guilty; not of felony malicious injury to property but of "*FELONY STUPIDITY*". No one could argue that! That is for certain! She closed by saying, something to the effect, "Her client had learned his lesson." The judge wasn't as amused as I was.

Our guy pled guilty and was sentenced; no trial. He received supervised felony probation with a 4-year prison sentence hanging over his head. He was also ordered to pay restitution for damages and spent 30 days in jail with work release. His mug shot was taken with him in his work shirt with his name and the company name he worked for in plain view on his chest. Nice!

The Rule: Don't break into a PI's office, or their house for that matter. They might just make you famous! If you sell used cars, stick to that!

As if all the above wasn't enough, Darren's rise to fame didn't end there. Word of the newspaper article with his picture spread through the media industry and we received a call from a TV producer. He was asking for permission to release the footage on his program. His show was called "World's Most Shocking And Dumbest Criminals". We obliged, and if you want to put on your own private detective hat, you'll no doubt find the footage from the show somewhere on the internet. If you want something to laugh over now; just relax and check out our YouTube channel, "The Private Dick Diaries".

Rule #3:

GIVE THE GUILTY PLENTY OF ROPE

I like to golf, a lot, and I play almost every day from when the snow leaves until it returns again. I'm actually getting better, which in this sport is amazing. Who knows, if I would have started before I turned 40 I might have had a different career! Regardless, it's become a big part of my life. Golf both relaxes and challenges me, and with what I do for a living it's become a critical part of my well-being. I even moved my family to a golf course after selling the acreage where we had our house on a mountain. I was spending way too much time just keeping up with the land and too little time with my family. Now I walk out my back door and golf with my kids! It's been a real blessing!

This story happened at Twin Lakes Village Golf Course, which just so happens to be the course I live on. At the time, I was on the Board of Directors. TLV is a residential community that has condominiums, townhomes, and custom homes, with quite a few of the residents being snow birds. It is hands down one of Idaho's most picturesque courses with great views of mountains and the lake, and the occasional morning moose crossing. It's a members' club but is open to the public as well. I had volunteered my expertise to install a top of the line security system. There is nowhere you can walk, inside or out, without being on camera. We had surveillance on the kitchen, the restaurant, the pool, the putting green, the carts, the bar, the outside seating, and, of course, the pro shop.

This particular incident happened on a usual Thursday, a pleasant spring day perfect for us golfers itching to get out on the courses and swing the clubs. A player came in and wanted to play a round of golf. Pro shop staff member, Matt, set him up and let him out right away with a twosome who happened to be members of the club. They finished playing and seemed to have had a nice game, at least from what I could see on the video. They said goodbye at the putting green, which is directly outside of the pro shop. Then the single player headed in to browse.

He decided to head out to the range to hit a bucket of balls and wanted to test drive a couple of the clubs. Not a problem, as this is fairly standard for golf shops; it's the try-it-then-buy-it policy. He paid five bucks cash for the bucket and, per protocol, gave a credit card in exchange for the clubs. As far as Matt knew he headed out to the range to hit a couple buckets and hopefully would like one of the clubs enough to buy it. It wasn't until Matt clocked in the next day that he realized this was not the case.

That morning I received a phone call from the head pro at the club.

"Hi Erin, can you come down to the club? We need to take a look at the security camera recordings." Then he gave me a brief rundown of the situation.

I, of course, agreed and stopped there on my way home from the office that night. We sat around the computer screen as I uploaded the footage. The only thing we knew was this man took clubs, left a credit card and never returned the clubs or picked up the card. It was only the head pro and the employee who talked to the guy. We began watching the film and it started just like the pro said; he was looking around at shoes, shirts, balls, gloves, then moved to the clubs. Nothing looked too suspicious. He didn't look around sneakily or anything like that. We watched him go to the counter, hand over his card, sign the cart log and leave with two top of the line, expensive clubs. It was when I switched to the outside camera view that it got quite a bit more interesting.

First let me describe the course layout so you can have a better understanding. The driving range is a short trip from the club house, but far enough that you need to take a cart if you want to get there with enough energy to actually swing a club or two. Our guy knew this and was told to grab a cart outside the clubhouse, which he signed for. They were there so they could be cleaned up and put away for the night and they already had keys in them. But as we continued watching the recording we noticed that *he walked right by the carts*. We have the occasional jock and exercise freak wanting to take the walk but he was not in that category. He was probably in his late 40's, old enough to know better, with light hair poking out under his Titleist hat, and stood a little under 5'7". He carried the majority of his weight in his gut, forcing him to keep his white pocket t-shirt un-tucked out of his army green cargo shorts. Not the physique you ever thought would take on the walk, so we watched as he started down the path with the demo clubs in his bag and carrying a bucket of balls. He walked a few more steps and without even a stumble he set the bucket down along the path and veered off to the parking lot! Nonchalantly, he put the clubs in his car and drove away!

I paused the recording, lowered my head, and then looked up to ask Darin the question I already knew the answer to.

"Let me guess, it wasn't his credit card he left, right?"

Not only was the card denied but Darin recognized the name on it! We finished playing the entire recording and shared it with the staff of the pro shop, as well as those who worked in the restaurant. No one recognized him. Darin called up a fellow head pro at another local course and threw out the name on the stolen card. Sure enough, it was his assistant pro, whom he quickly handed the phone to.

"Hi, this is Darin from Twin Lakes Village Golf Course. Someone was golfing with us yesterday and used *your* credit card to demo a couple of our clubs. Unfortunately, he never brought them back."

"*What card*?!"

He continued telling Darren that his '#*^@ ing" clubs were stolen almost two months ago and his wallet was in his golf bag. We invited him down to view the recording on the long-shot that our guy was stupid enough to steal from somewhere he frequented, enough to be recognized by the employees. Well, it turned out he was, indeed, this stupid as he was identified by name the moment his face turned into our surveillance camera!

Perfect. We had a name, "John," and we had a crime. Time to turn over all the details to the authorities and let them do their thing. Or so we thought....

It was pretty cut and dried so I considered my job done and left it at that. It wasn't until I received a phone call from Darin *months* down the road that I found out this was not the case. He had heard nothing from the officer after our first discussion, the day after we gave our report. I just so happened to be on a stakeout on a different case when Darin called. I was sitting in my car enjoying a cup of coffee and patiently waiting for another subject to make a move out of their house. Nothing had happened for the last 4 hours so I assumed I'd have time to take this call, but I was sorry I did as it was a real mood changer.

Darin told me this excuse for an officer of the law decided on his own merits the incident in question was all just a big misunderstanding, and he said our thief would bring or send the clubs back using UPS. I was livid! Apparently, he was convinced enough that he completely forgot and wrote off the "alleged" stolen credit card. I immediately hung up from talking to the "detective" and called Darin back.

"Can you get me this John's phone number? Maybe call that pro?" I asked.

Within the half hour Darin called me back with a cell phone number. This guy was guilty of not only burglary but theft too. I wasn't ready to let him get off that easy- especially at *my* club. Nothing was happening as of yet at my stakeout, so I decided this was as good a time as any to give John a call myself. So I plugged my handy little recorder microphone into my cell, put on the earpiece, and started to punch in his numbers.

Before I get too far into the conversation, don't worry I'll detail it all out for you, it's important to share another valuable skill I have learned over the years. I've taken *numerous* courses and spent *years* learning the tactics when it comes to suspect interrogation and it proved most beneficial for this case. But this skill is not nearly as effective without also being well-versed in reading individual personality and communication styles, which has also taken me multiple years to perfect. This is 100% true, and if you take the time to study it can be priceless. When you can determine which personality quadrant someone falls into you can better communicate with the individual by speaking their same language. I use this when I deal with anyone I come into contact with; I even use it on my wife and kids. There are four basic types and we all fall primarily into one. It helps with my family and friends and my business relationships.

Which man or woman out there wouldn't want to learn how to better communicate with their spouse? Naturally my motivation and intent are completely opposite if I'm using it to interrogate a suspect versus figuring out my wife's latest mood switch, but the theory is the same. All I have to do is ask enough proper questions to bring out that person's style, and then I've got them.

This is what happened during this call, and it was *beautiful.*

One ring…two rings…three rings…four rings…five rings…

"Hello"

"Hello, is John there?"

"This is John."

"John, this is Erin Jenkins. I'm with Twin Lakes Village. I'm on the Board of Directors there."

"Yeah."

"We've got some videos of you, uh, taking a couple of our clubs and I'd like to have those clubs back, John."

"They are back."

"Oh, they are?"

"Yeah, I sent them back yesterday. There was no intention there, it uh, um, I just kinda panicked on a bad situation and made it worse. That's just not me."

"Oh, I didn't know that."

"Yeah, I sent them back yesterday or the day before."

"So you weren't intentionally trying to steal our clubs?"

"Hell no!"

"Are you telling me that you didn't mean to take our clubs?"

"No, no" (insert clumsy giggle). "I actually work at Twin Lakes. I'm the guy who cleans the pool there. I'm sure you guys have seen me. I was golfing there that day. Um, yah…I sent them back by UPS and the officer said they have received them already. There was no intention at all I just um, um kinda panicked because of the situation with the, you know, using the wrong card and all."

"Ok, so…"

"Yeah, I sent them back and put a little note in there you know with the date that I took them out and I said I was sorry and all that kinda crap. And, um, I truly am sorry."

"The fact that you gave Matt a stolen credit card..."

"Oh, yeah that, I explained to the officer that that wasn't on purpose either."

"How do you end up with a stolen credit card, John? I just gotta know. You don't just end up with a stolen credit card from a local golf pro."

"Yeah, um well, someone's after me, I was telling the officer, it was a hell of a day. I had some incidents in the past and the same groups of people are after me again. Like this past summer I've had notes in my mail box that they're "going to get me" and false claims from other golf courses that aren't true; they're one hundred percent not true. I told all this to the sergeant. Even the Prairie Falls thing where they falsely accused me and all I wanted to do was make it right. I returned all the clubs they said were missing, paying out of my own pocket. He just didn't believe me, didn't believe me at all, so that's his opinion."

"Okay, okay so I got a question for you, just to satisfy my curiosity."

"Sure."

"How do you end up with a stolen credit card in your wallet? And then you pull it out to use, cause I got some great video of you."

"Yeah I know, I know, I actually talked to the guy…"

"You even signed the name from the card."

"Um, uh, no I think I signed my name."

"Nope, you signed his; I've got the check-out sheet. So how do you spin that one around John?"

"Is *my* name on that sheet?"

"Nope, you're name isn't, but the name from the stolen credit card is."

"No, I'm pretty sure I signed my name and paid cash for the game, I'm pretty sure."

"Okay, here's the deal. I'm going to cut to the chase. I can live with "oh gee I made a mistake and I shouldn't have done that" but I'm not buying your story because the video I have is quite different."

"Uh, well…um"

"I can live with all that, but what I can't live with is the B#! S#!*!!, because it is BS."*

"It's not BS, it's…"

"It is BS and one and one don't add up and it's really starting to piss me off. So did you: A – actually knowingly steal some clubs and use a stolen credit card but now feel remorseful for it, or B- the BS you're trying to fling? Be careful because your answer will determine where I go from here."

"Well, I…"

"Be careful, because if you stick to your lies I will go down to the prosecutor's myself and pound on his desk until he takes you down. You tell me the truth and I may have some mercy on you. But it's starting to really piss me off, so which is it?"

The long silent pause came across to me *loud and clear*.

"Okay, I'm going to give it to you straight. I see that's how you are and I appreciate that, that honesty of yours, I'm the same way. It was an honest mistake, one hundred percent mistake, and it won't happen again."

"You used a stolen credit card and signed a false name and that was an honest mistake! Is that what you want me to believe? Is it John?"

"Well… I was drunk. We all were, I started before I even got here and just kept going."

"You were what?"

"I was just in the wrong place at the wrong time, I've had a rough few months. I was involved in a shooting and my medications aren't all working. There are just a lot, a lot of little things going on. I told the officer I just want to make it right, if I have to pay for the clubs or..."

"I'm going to tell you how you can make it right, right now. And that's to tell me the truth. Don't jack me around with "I was drunk, I was this, I was that" cause that's starting to really, really piss me off. If you have the balls to tell me that you did this stuff and you're sorry for it I can live with that."

"I'm not going to bullshit you, like I said I'm one hundred percent sorry."

"I'm sure you're sorry. I'm absolutely sure of that. But don't tell me it was an honest mistake, because I can't buy that!"

"Let me finish, let me finish. I know you're frustrated so let me answer a few of your questions. I lost my credit card on the course. I told the officer that, so I used this other one and signed the false name but it was never my intention to steal. I panicked, I panicked and just left and I made a mistake. I've got a lot of remorse and it'll never happen again. I work there, well I do work there, and it doesn't look good for the company. I told my boss and my wife and I'm trying to man up on this and take my medicine, you know what I get. You know if I can't play there anymore, whatever it is."

I could see he had grabbed the rope so I just kept silent and let him continue to hang himself with it.

"I gotta make a life change here, it was a stupid act and I'm willing to do whatever you think I need to do to make it right."

"So, you're wanting me to believe that you took the clubs using a credit card that wasn't yours, which is theft and forgery by the way, you went to the driving range for a bit then just threw them in your car and drove off, without bringing them back. Is that right?"

"Yep, yah. I didn't intend on stealing them I was going to bring them back."

"Bull! You've got one more time to come clean. There is no way, without us having this video, you would have never have returned these clubs. I know that and you know that's the truth. So what is it? What's the truth, John?"

"No, I was…"

"Give me a break. I'm not an idiot, we would never have seen those clubs again and you know that."

"I would never call you an idiot; I know you're not one. Honest to God..."

"Let's leave Him out of this, don't even go there with me. I'm not buying it, you stole the clubs and you had no intention of bringing them back. Isn't that right, John?"

Another perfectly telling pause, then a loose attempt to change the direction only tightened his noose.

"How'd you get my number anyways?"

"That's not the issue here."

"It doesn't matter, I'm glad you called; we need to get this ironed out."

"We'll get it ironed out all right, but how I go about it really depends on you. You own up to it, forget this other crap, and finally just tell me the truth. Or we're going to the prosecutor and pound on his desk until he nails you to the wall. We will not let this go until you're buried! But on the other hand, if you want to come clean... maybe, just maybe..."

This was the longest and *most significant* gap in our entire conversation. I could tell the tides were about to change.

"Well...the truth is...I went in there to demo the clubs, I gave the wrong credit card, signed his name, I panicked and left and was not at that time intending to bring them back. Then I started to have second thoughts, I really was."

"You didn't intend on bringing them back?"

"No, not that day. But the day or so after I started to feel real guilty and wanted to bring them back."

"Okay."

"That's the truth."

"Okay, okay that's the truth. So let me reiterate this one more time, just so I can get it right. You admit that you took two demo clubs from Twin Lakes Village Golf Course and did not intend on bringing them back. Is that what you're saying?"

"Yes."

"I can buy that. And you did know that you used a stolen credit card and that you did realize that you signed a name other than yours?"

"Yes."

"Well, John I appreciate that. I'm going to let the rest of the Board know that you did indeed own up to the facts and that we've got our clubs back. Are

you willing to come into the club and make an apology to the Board? Are you willing to do that John?"

"Yes."

"So I'm going to tell the Board that you are willing to come in and confess that you knowingly took two of our demo clubs, using a stolen credit card, forged a false name, and had no intention of bringing them back. Is that correct?"

"Yes, yes that's right."

"Okay John, I'll let you know how it goes."

"Okay, thanks."

Click…click.

Twenty minutes later our call was done and luckily nothing had happened to the house I was watching on stakeout. I immediately hung up and redialed the call I made prior to this one. I informed the officer that I not only had an admission of guilt, but I also had it recorded and he should be in my office tomorrow morning so he could reopen this case. The officer never showed….

Three days later, I got a call from Darin telling me this *same cop* showed up! He wanted to get the note John had sent with the clubs, because he was reopening the case since HE got a confession from John! What this brilliant man in blue didn't know was I had been at the pro shop the day after I spoke with John, and shared my recorded call with all of the employees at TLV.

"You have got to listen to this. It's hilarious!"

Then I also told them to be sure to share it with the entire staff from the course where he initially stole the credit card- and they did. Darin is probably one of the most polite people I have ever met, so I wasn't surprised when he simply said nothing while letting the officer continue to falsely toot his own horn.

I was asked a while ago exactly what John had said that triggered me into knowing what personality quadrant he fit into. To someone like myself who has spent years studying these things, it is truly an amazing *ah-ha* moment when you know you've got someone pegged in the right slot. John's give-away was the way he responded to me. He tried to make me believe that we were the same when he said, "I see that's how you are and I appreciate that, that honesty of yours, I'm the same way." Hook, line and sinker!

I knew he was a con man. He really was quite an expert at convincing people that he was a decent person, and even had our officer hooked! I knew the minute he tried to pull that on me that he was a man of little integrity with no conscience. He needs to have others think highly of him. That's when I knew how to feed him; I was able to bring out his true side and it was obvious by the end of our conversation. I've also been asked why he just didn't hang up when he caught on. The beauty is that he never really caught on until it was *too late*. He needed to play the game as that's how he gets his kicks. It's similar to wealthy people who shoplift; it's not the take it's the game that they're after. John just never came across an opponent who knew the right string to pull, at the right time, to get the truth.

The pro whose card was in the stolen golf bag heard the recording and immediately called me, impressed. He asked me to find out if it was, indeed, John who stole his clubs. After I told him that the odds were against us of finding that out considering how much time had lapsed, and along with my daily fee, he politely declined. Not sure he would have pursued it if it hadn't been so long ago. My fee probably would have come close to a new set of clubs, and according to him he got enough satisfaction listening to me "work him over" on the recording!

John was arrested that afternoon.

I called the prosecutor and when we first talked I asked if he wanted a copy of the recorded confession. This surprised him as the police report stated that it was *the officer* who had gotten the confession. Too bad the cop didn't have any integrity either.

"Really? Does he have a recording of it?", I asked the prosecutor. That set the story straight...

It was determined from talking to the other golf courses John had made a lucrative income stealing and selling clubs online. With this information, and an unarguable confession, a plea of guilty no contest ended the case. He was sentenced to a year in prison and paid a fine of $127.00. But worse than this, especially for a golfer, our recording went viral throughout the industry and John has been *banned* from any and all courses in Northern Idaho and Eastern Washington!

The Rule: If you clean swimming pools at golf resorts for a job, that is a respectable way to make a living. Although you might be smarter than the local detective, you are not smarter than the golf pro or PI who lives there!

Want a little taste of the actual recording? Check it out on our "YouTube" Channel: The Private Dick Diaries: "Real Life Confession Gathered By A PI".

Rule #4:

DON'T ASSUME ALL THAT GLITTERS IS THE SAME GOLD

If you own a television or a radio, you know that more and more experts recommend gold for investments over almost any other resource, especially the US dollar. That alone makes this case high profile, therefore we will not be using any proper name, which includes the company. Suffice it to say this corporation is a *major* player in the gold and fine metals community with mines throughout multiple states, as well as Canada and many other foreign countries. Let's just call it "The Gold Company".

The Gold Company is much more complex than a few bearded men with picks and shovels hoping to strike it rich. It is an elaborate and well thought out corporation which has the process of mining perfected better than most of its competitors. The process from dirt to gold is quite intricate. It requires multiple pieces of equipment which are, as you can imagine, extremely expensive.

This is a basic description in layman's terms of gold mining procedures. First, before anything can start, there has to be some inkling that there is actually “gold in them thar hills,” I know some of our readers are probably less interested in how gold is processed and probably more fascinated if we were talking about a diamond mine, but remember, most of those sparkly rocks are set in gold.

Once gold is determined to be present, extraction begins; using some of those large pricey machines. They start to grind away rock and move soil until the pockets of gold are found. Once this drilling is complete the mine shaft is built to encompass the gold pockets. Next comes recovery; the rocks and dirt with gold is extracted from the mine. From here the rocks are crushed into fine powder and then mixed with a solution to create sludge. The sludge is stored in tanks and mixed with a clarifier and, finally, pushed through a filter where the gold is separated from the liquid and recovered.

Remember, this is an *extremely* dumbed-down description. In order to explain it in its fullest would take ten pages and would need complicated flow charts mentioning equipment: vibrating feeders, jaw crushers, ball mills, dryers, floatation machines, magnetic separators and spiral classifiers. However, we were concerned with the mixers, more specifically the stainless steel rods in the vats that did the mixing.

After many years of mixing, these rods become impregnated with gold particles that are worth *millions* of dollars! A local chemist was fortunate and brilliant enough to come up with a chemical process that removes impregnated gold from various other metals; one being, of course, stainless steel. The Gold Company heard of this and immediately contacted the chemist (which is what he'll be known as throughout the story – remember no names) and after coming to an *extremely* lucrative deal, they shredded these rods into a steel wool type of material.

Millions of dollars were at stake, so the gold came with a full security team. It was delivered in armored trucks and the Gold Company virtually took over the chemist's facility. Door locks were changed, security cameras were installed and there were guards on the premise 24/7. This job lasted almost one month, and everyday started and ended with full head to toe searches making certain everything was on the up and up. The chemist would run the wool through multiple tubes flushing it with his special formula. Then the metal was tested and if there were still gold remnants left they would flush them through the piping again; as many times as it took until all the gold was recovered. Naturally, no one other than the chemist knew the ideal chemical combination, which is why he could ask for virtually any fee he wanted! The Gold Company would gladly pay considering it was wasted gold until they heard about the chemist's discovery; to them it was all bonus money. Needless to say, they paid him a healthy sum, along with a few gold nuggets.

Eight months or so had gone by; a long time since the security guards and armored trucks left the chemist's lab. The job was done and forgotten… almost. The skill of the chemist to remove gold from various metals spread through the industry and caught the attention of a local miner. This miner was, for lack of a better word, "minor" compared to The Gold Company. He had a small mine up in the hills of Idaho and did his prospecting by hand versus the multi-million dollar pieces of equipment. Regardless of size, he too wanted to maximize his gold retention, so he hired the chemist to remove gold from his tailings. Tailings are basically the crushed and milled rock residue left after mineral extraction. The major mining companies have equipment that can successfully do this for them, but smaller miners find it hard to get that detailed by hand. He took his tailings in, and within a few weeks was rewarded with a gold nugget about the size of a plum pit. Not a bad take for a little miner since, considering once again, it was gold he wouldn't have had without the chemist's help.

The miner wanted to know the exact value of his nugget so he enlisted the help of another metal specialist, an alchemist. The definition of an alchemist has progressed over time; it stems from the middle ages where scientists attempted to make gold from metals. The process involved taking something worthless and changing it into something valuable. It combined chemistry with philosophy, and in the years of its origin alchemists were considered healing men with mystical powers. The definition has evolved somewhat since those times, and now is used to simply describe an individual who is well-versed in the metal industry. They can take a gold or silver nugget and not only determine its purity, but also *its origin.*

Each mine has its own stamp of characteristics depending on the composites in the earth; no two mines are alike. As you can imagine, this profession is a rare one and only those who do it extremely well are still in business. One particular alchemist is located in Northern Idaho and is proficient in both gold and silver. He is well acquainted with gold and is able to distinguish from a sample the exact location of the mine from where it was extracted! Quite interesting, really, that so many details can be determined from a simple piece of ore! What the alchemist found in our local miner's nugget was also very interesting:

"Where'd you get this nugget?" The alchemist's question obviously surprised the miner.

"From my mine."

"No you didn't. I know this gold and it's definitely not from your mine."

The alchemist was able to determine it was indeed not from the miner's mine, but was, in fact, from one of the mines belonging to The Gold Company! This was more than a bit suspicious, so the local miner put a call into The Gold Company and was referred to the head of security. We'll call him Tony. After hearing the story, Tony was equally suspicious and immediately took the matter into his own hands. Both parties were invested in finding out the truth as both were being taken by the chemist, and they had to get to the bottom of things. That's how we came into play.

I was the first phone call Tony made after hearing the local miner's predicament. He was familiar with Confidential Investigations and knew that I'd be able to help him out. I'll admit I was very intrigued; nothing like a theft case to get the juices flowing.

This was going to be fun and I knew exactly where to start. The local gold buyers may have some information that would help our investigation. We mapped out the dealers within the vicinity of the chemist's lab and decided to pop in and do some inquiring. I told Tony to let me take the lead as we entered the first store on our list. I asked for the owner, who just so happened to be the man that greeted us upon entering. He was friendly enough during our initial chit-chat, but got less helpful the more I inquired about the chemist and their association with one another.

"So you do know him. Great, can I see his records of what was sold to you?"

"I'm not showing you anything."

Damn, we almost had it; guess I get to play a little hard ball.

"Ok, no problem, but let me tell you what's going to happen. He's been stealing from The Gold Company and when I get proof, because I will, I'm coming after you for receiving stolen property."

He got us the records.

According to the data he had sold close to thirty thousand dollars worth of gold to this dealer over the past eight months. We couldn't be sure if it was all stolen from The Gold Company but he had no records that dated before the job he did for them, so we had the impression that it was. But I still had one more thought I needed to put into the buyer's head before we could leave.

"Here's the deal. I know that you and the chemist are close, probably even friends, considering all the business he's done with you. But if you so much as hint to him that we were here..."

"No, no I wouldn't do that."

"If I find out you did, when he gets charged I'll make certain you're standing right next to him for receiving stolen property. Got it?"

He did, and it was obvious how scared he was by the trembling of his hand when we shook goodbye. He wasn't telling anyone we talked, I was certain of that. I was also fairly certain he had plenty of skeletons in his closet and didn't want the likes of a PI poking around him or his business!

It was time to get ahold of the chemist and see what we could shake out of him. Tony gave him a call to make an appointment. The chemist was more than accommodating. My guess was that he was hopeful The Gold Company wanted to make another deal - and they did, sort of. Tony told him that we were only in town a few more days and the chemist agreed to meet us at our hotel's conference room. He didn't have to know we weren't actually staying there or that I wasn't officially an employee of The

Gold Company! All he needed to know was we wanted to talk to him.

Tony and I prepared a little good-cop, bad-cop, scenario before he met with us. He showed up on time and was clearly excited by whatever possibilities he had imagined. We did our introductions and sat down at the conference table. He immediately started sharing how he had refined the process since the last job and went on and on – blah blah blah – about how hard he'd been working on it and anxious to do it for us again. I knew immediately after meeting him exactly the type of person we were dealing with. I let him rattle on, just long enough for me to pinpoint his personality style in order to communicate with him and ultimately get the confession we had come for. Now it was time to hit him with the big guns, and shoot the air out of his balloon of hope.

"Well, before we get much further into this we need to discuss an issue from the last job you did." I purposively paused a little longer than I normally would have just so I could observe his reaction. I could definitely see the wheels turning.

"We're missing a bunch of gold from that job." I said. Again, another pause, but this time he was the one who paused, not me.

"What do you mean?" He finally managed to stumble out.

"Gold from that mine is starting to show up in unlikely places; any idea why?"

"So you're not here to hire me?" Another visible stumble.

"Hell no, you'll probably never be hired again by anyone." Tony was quick to interject and it was obvious we had him on the line.

"I think I want to call my lawyer."

"Probably a good idea, but before you do, let me tell you how this is going to go. I've got proof that you stole and its *well* within the *felony range*." (In this state that's anything over $1,000.) "I'm going to go down to the Sheriff's office today with what I have and they are going to arrest you…today. Then you can get your lawyer and have him attempt to do his magic."

As much as I was enjoying watching the blood run out of his face, Tony was getting even more pleasure out of it. He stood up to join me, and I could see his enthusiasm and wanted to make certain he didn't get too anxious before we got what we needed. We now knew the chemist was guilty, but how guilty was yet to be determined. Tony was playing his part perfectly, and I jumped up in front of him to make it look like I was "saving" the chemist from his wrath.

"Here's your one chance. You come clean now and tell us how much you took. Then we're going to go to your lab and get whatever you have left, then you're going to pay it all back to The Gold Company. Plus you're going to pay what it cost for us (I pointed to Tony and myself) to do this investigation. Is that clear?"

My glance towards Tony was enough to let him know that now was the time to stay still and quiet. Tony and I both returned to our seats that were directly across the table from the chemist. The chemist dropped his head, and as his shoulders slumped forward he quietly responded:

"I sold about $30,000 and still have a little left."

That was what we needed and now it was time to head over to his lab. He obliged willingly. Tony and I followed him as he pulled out of the hotel parking lot in his relatively new loaded 4x4 truck. Tony then told me the chemist had 2 kids and guessed they were still in elementary school, and a wife that was involved in numerous charitable events in the area. I just shook my head in disgust. I couldn't wrap my head around the fact that he didn't have to put his family through the hell heading their way. He made plenty of cash, obviously had lots of nice things, and there was no reason for him to steal. Well, nothing except greed.

We entered his facility which was vacant and dark. He flicked on the switch and took us through a mini tutorial as we walked towards a back room. This room housed a garbage bag half-full of tailings. He told us that this was all he had left from The Gold Company job; he had sold everything else.

"We had security around the clock 24/7. How did you manage to get away with all of this?"

The chemist knew he had been busted, so proceeded to tell us that security *thought* the entire residue was flushed through the piping, but what he did not tell them was a good amount of sediment settled in the ridges of the tubes even *after* it had been flushed. This is what he decided to keep for himself! This is what the crime was; he knowingly kept gold that was not his and held back valuable information.

The chemist gave all of this up very willingly, which led me to believe he may not be telling me the whole truth. Tony happened to have the same feeling and decided to step in. Fortunately he knew the bad cop tactic, playing hard ball to a tee, and he came down hard on the chemist trying to squeeze the entire truth out of him. He stepped in front of him and puffed up his already enormous chest as a scare tactic.

"I…I'm not sure I want you guys in here anymore." The chemist said.

That was my cue to step in between the two of them and reel our criminal back in. Most people would have crushed under Tony's burley thumb, but not someone with the personality style of our chemist. He only responded to facts not idle threats so, as planned, I brought him back into his comfort zone.

"Look, do you want to make this hard or make it easy? Because it could get ugly, really ugly. You need to tell us the rest."

This brought him back and we were once again in control and, as planned, Tony stepped aside to let me back in the driver's seat.

"We are going to walk away today with all you have left and while we're bagging it up you need to think about what road you want to take, cuz it is up to you. Hard or less hard? You know we have you so that being fact, what do you want to do from here?"

The chemist thought for less than a minute and then quietly spoke. "Ok, ok."

There is nothing sweeter than the taste of victory, and when his shoulders slumped forward and he dropped his head, I knew we had won! We all walked towards the table and took a seat. I told him I was going to record our conversation and he silently agreed. I legally needed to have his consent as we were in Washington State. In Idaho, the laws are different and the second party does not need to be made aware of the recording. I set the recorder in the middle of the table and hit the button.

"No…I don't think I want to do this." He was wafting again and I needed to react quickly.

"Ok your choice." I clicked off the recorder, picked up my cell and started dialing random numbers hoping he'd take the bait.

"You're right; let's let the authorities deal with this." I said.

"What, what do mean?" He took the bait.

"We should have just called the sheriff in the first place, they'll be here within the hour and we'll do it by the book. They'll handcuff you and we'll go from there." That's all he needed to hear and we were back in business.

"No, let's do it this way." He said.

The recorder went back on the table and he began from the beginning. When he was done he took an abnormally deep breath, the kind most of us take out of relief. I was hoping, for his sake, that being relieved at this point was not what he was thinking because his hell had just gotten started!

"How are you going to pay back the 30 grand?" This question brought him back to his new reality.

"I'll have to work on that."

"We're in town for only one more day, so you figure it out and we'll have a signed agreement tomorrow before we leave." Another stretch of the truth but it was all part of the plan.

We left him still sitting at the table slumped over in his thoughts. I assured Tony that he was not a flight risk. Where was he going to run to? He had a wife, kids, a business (well at least for the time being) and a huge house.

The next day arrived and when Tony returned to my office I placed a call to the chemist to set up the meeting. There was a slight change, however. The chemist asked us to meet him at his attorney's office. Tony wasn't as enthusiastic as I was about the adjustment because he didn't know that I have spent *plenty* of time dealing with lawyers, and they do not intimidate me in the least.

Tony put a call into The Gold Company's attorneys, but I assured them a trip over here was not necessary as I had things under control. They weren't very convinced, but with a recommendation from Tony they agreed to let us go at it alone. Great! This was going to be fun!

We walked into the prestigious offices of "Dewey Cheatem & How" (old lawyer joke) and the games began. I deliberately said nothing as we courteously shook hands and made the appropriate introductions. We sat in an elaborate marbled conference room and the chemist's attorney opened up with what he thought would be his verbal tackle, which might have worked if we weren't holding the cards.

"My client is not guilty; therefore, you will not be receiving anything today." He said.

The head of security looked my way and waited for my rebuttal.

"So, what you're saying is that your client did not steal $30,000?" I asked.

He nodded, to which I responded by pulling the recorder out of my jacket pocket and proceeded to hit the play button. I had, of course, conveniently preset the recorder to the exact moment of his client's confession.

"If that's the stand you're taking then we're out of here and you can stop wasting my time." I then stood and ventured towards the door. Another bait set.

"Now just wait a minute…" And (another) bait taken.

We walked back to the table and before I sat down I made my outcome of the meeting known.

"We either get a deal done on paper today or your client is in handcuffs." I stated.

His attorney was more than blinded by the turn of events and this became apparent as he tried to rein things back in.

"If you think you can pull that off." He said.

"*I don't think, I know*." I grabbed my phone and once again started to dial unknown random numbers. I could read this guy already and he was one hundred percent going to cave.

"Let's talk about this…" He pleaded.

It's a shame sometimes how much amusement I get out of my job. His so-called *lion of an attorney* had become a lamb and we were the Shepherds. Time to get down to business and seal this deal!

"I'll talk, you listen. We'll have our 30 grand tonight or his ass is in jail, and he'll spend well over 30k for his defense." Good, his attention was where I needed it to be and the floor was all mine. I smiled and sat down in front of a legal pad and laid out the terms.

I knew that leaving with the entire thirty thousand was not realistic, but it was necessary to make my point, and to appear as if I was giving an inch. So I began to write as I verbally told them our terms. We agreed if, and only if, we left today with $10,000 in good faith and he agreed to pay the balance, plus our fee, in full within 30 days.

"You can't tack things on," His attorney said in an attempt to get some control back.

"Do I have to go over this again?" I glanced at Tony with a "haven't we been here before" look?

The attorney looked at his client and nodded. We left with a recorded agreement and a promise of $10,000 from the attorney's trust account by end of business day.

Tony made a call to The Gold Company to fill them in on the details as we drove back to the hotel. When Tony initially talked with the company president his request was to throw the thief in jail but we convinced them that while they could go that route, chances were they'd never see their money. They could either have him arrested or get him to repay the cash, but they couldn't have both.

Tony was impressed with the entire case, especially how we played the attorney like a fiddle. His only request was to have a copy of the recording to share with his boss.

As it played out, over the next few months the chemist's business partner agreed to pay off the chemist's debt.

No charges were filed per the agreement and our client regained their losses, plus expenses.

The Rule: Don't think that just because you have a slick attorney things are going to go your way. Slick only works when you have the facts on your side. Just pay up and move on, and don't waste my time!

Rule #5:

DON'T OVERLOOK EVEN THE SMALLEST OF CLUES

When we take on a case we make it a habit to know what our goal is as well as what outcome the client desires. Hopefully the two match. But every once in a while the end result is not what was expected at all. This is one such case. It started as a child custody investigation but turned into *so much more*.

Tina was married to Luke, and from the outside they seemed happy and content just like many other wed couples. They had a family together with two girls, and a boy who was the eldest. Luke worked hard every day and Tina was a stay-at-home mom taking care of the house and kids. It looked like a complete picture of happiness but to Tina something was missing. She began to see the day in and day out ritual as being painful chores and was craving adult interaction. Unfortunately, the something she thought she was missing and the interaction she was longing for was found in the arms and the bed of a much younger man.

She had a romantic affair that ended after only a few months. Unfortunately, it also left Tina with a *baby* on the way! From first glance one could see what the attraction might have been. Dale was the high school football star and other than a substantial mid-section he managed to retain some of his boyish good looks; along with an "I'm so awesome" ego. Tina was ten years his senior so the attention from a younger man was what filled the absence she was feeling in her marriage. Tina, too, had retained her youthful look and had a figure that most women in their 20's envied. They had met, ironically, on a girl's night out when Luke had convinced Tina to get out and have some fun while he stayed home and cared for the children. I'm certain this wasn't the fun he was referring too. It started as playful flirting but quickly moved into inappropriate behavior under the darkened bar lights. Numbers were exchanged and Tina found herself calling Dale within the week. He was more than eager to meet up with her again.

All affairs start under the radar and some even stay hidden, but eventually the truth will always prevail. In this case the truth was going to appear as it grew right in front of everyone including her husband. This affair was a mistake which carried much more than just shame and embarrassment; they would have a constant reminder of her indiscretion. After many months of what I could only imagine were in-depth heated discussions, Luke and Tina decided their marriage was strong enough to overcome her infidelity. Luke was a better man than most and willingly volunteered to take on this child as his own son.

For the most part, it seemed as life was attempting to get back to normal for this family until 18 months after the birth of the baby. Dale, along with his excuse for a mother, decided they were going to fight for custody. As disrespectful and insolent as Dale was, he looked like a saint next to his mom! She had no concept of proper human behavior; in her mind she was a victim of society and expected everything from everyone for nothing. She had no manners to speak of, and would frequently harass Luke and Tina with drive-by bellows and telephone berating. It was her persistent harassing that finally convinced Luke it was time to deal with this once and for all.

As if a deranged Grandmother wasn't cause enough to fight this custody request, Dale had a semi-undercover occupation that didn't exactly qualify him for "daddy of the year". Under his Uncle's wing he was following in the family business and learning the fine art of drug running across the Canadian border. His uncle had his hand slapped by the law. They just couldn't make anything major stick enough to put him out of business. So he decided to lay low and take more of a managerial role and let his nephew risk the foot work. Sadly,

Tina knew this when she hooked up with him and chose to ignore it.

Regardless of how they arrived at the situation today, there was no way in hell Luke was going to let this deadbeat or his mother anywhere near this child. Luke had a good job that he had been at for a very long time and not so much as a sneeze with the law. He had a proven track record of providing for his family and was a stellar citizen in the community. Unfortunately, not being the boy's biological father was going to be a tough connection to break legally. They needed help and originally went to the Sheriff's department with their complaints. According to an employee there, they were "too busy" to take it on and recommended another agency. That's where Confidential Investigations came into play. It was a bit surprising we were the direction they steered them considering we had recently busted some not-so-law-abiding officers on their force. Guess they were convinced we knew our stuff.

Luke made an appointment and as he laid the story out for me I couldn't help but ask myself, "If I were him, would I be man enough to take this same stand?" Even though Dale and his mommy were pushing for custody they really would settle for visitation, which until this time Dale had not been granted. Luke needed to ensure this never happened, and wanted the sperm donor to simply disappear.

To guarantee this we would have to do everything in our investigative power to not only prove Dale an unfit father, but to also demonstrate that he would be a threat to the well-being of this child! We needed to expose his drug trafficking ways and have substantial proof, not just here-say and rumors that were out there. I'll admit that I let my emotions take over a bit as I listened to Luke and his pleas. He was this child's father regardless of where the DNA came from. He was committed to the well-being of this child and in my mind that was the definition of a parent. In his guidance this child had a chance to grow and make something for himself in the future. Luke was determined not to let the child pay for the mistakes of the adults. I respected him for this and wanted to help.

We started our investigation by pulling an elaborate background check on Dale. This report included addresses of all previous and present residences, jobs he had held in the past, current employment, any trouble with the law, as well as his detailed financial information. It showed that he currently owned a house, had no legal troubles not even a speeding ticket, held a few odd jobs but no current employment was listed, yet *ironically* he had plenty of cash. He drove around in a newer white Ford

350 Diesel truck with a logo on the doors marketing him as a contractor, even though we knew he had never built anything in his life. What we did know was that his Uncle had the exact same logo on his truck, and as far as we could tell he, too, had nothing to show to confirm the legitimacy of this business. We had called the number from the truck numerous times and were always left with a friendly female's voice telling us that he was not available and that she would gladly take a message for him. It was time to do some deeper investigating.

We put a tail on him and spent the next few days following him around to see if there were any patterns or unusual behaviors. The house that was in his name was quite impressive, even for someone who had a job. It was in a prestigious neighborhood near the lake and was grand in both size and appearance. Made primarily of brick with cedar accents it sat on a larger than average lot and was well kept. It was not the kind of house one would assume he lived in, especially after meeting him. We camped out a couple of days and recorded all license plates of the *many* visitors that travelled in and out of his driveway. It was a busy place, to say the least, and the only repeat guests were that of the current high school football coach and another friend who we found out was named Willy. The coach apparently was living there with Dale which caused all sorts of red flags to wave. The others were mostly high school students and football players who only added to the flag parade. He had to be dealing drugs out of the house but we needed more than the obvious perceptions. Luke and Tina only had one shot to rid them of Dale and we needed to have undeniable proof of his druggy ways. We had to keep digging, and for this we needed Tina's help.

Tina was not the kind of woman anyone would pair up with Dale, but who knows what the allure was when they first met. They seemed to have fed each other's needs at the time. Tina was enjoying the attention of a younger man and Dale was proud to show off his good looking "Cougar" of a girlfriend. Fortunately for us, Dale also liked to boast about the success he was having with his profession and, without knowing it, had exposed Tina to the complete ins and outs of the process. She had spent plenty of time around Dale and his partners-in-crime so she was in a position to tell us not only who, but what, where and when as well!

We invited a detective from the drug task force to sit in on our meeting with Tina. We were going to need their help if we were hoping of turning our findings into arrests. It's actually a great partnership; we can investigate in ways when the police force's hands are tied, yet we can't make legal arrests for the crimes we uncover. Some police understand this and we have a great working relationship with them; others aren't willing to see the big picture and are threatened by us (or scared of us considering some of our recent investigations against them). It's too bad, really, considering the possibilities. This individual knew the benefits of working together and was more than thrilled to be invited to sit in. She and her team had heard these names flying around in the past, but until now had no way to penetrate their inner circle.

Tina started by confirming Willy as his right-hand man and named two others who were usually involved in the border diversion. Willy was not clean like Dale. He had numerous run-ins with the local and federal law enforcements and was currently on probation for drug trafficking. He was a scrawny punk low-life and this would be enough to put him away for good, and trust me, this kind of "POS" would be pretty popular behind bars. She then continued on and detailed their border runs step by step.

Dale would rent a car from a local rental place and always choose the border crossings that were set up in the middle of basically nowhere. These po-dunk border crossings typically had two shack-like buildings, one on one side of the imaginary country line and one mirror imaged on the other side. Two flags flew high above each building; this side was a US flag and an Idaho state flag, the others were a Canadian flag and a British Columbia provincial flag. They chose these crossings for their obvious quietness and lack of steady traffic. British Columbia was the province of choice, because of its marijuana growth potential and ocean access which allowed for unlimited buying sources.

Dale, Willy and the other two cohorts would drive towards the border together. Dale would stop on the US side shy of the border patrol and drop off all three passengers. He would legally cross the boundary alone as the others quietly snuck across the line under the noses of both countries. Then they would have a meeting spot safely on the other side where Dale would pick them up and they'd be on their way. After they had made the B.C. bud pickup, they would simply repeat the procedure only with backpacks loaded with their purchases.

According to Tina, he had been doing this since high school when Dale's uncle used to be the driver and Dale was the runner. Apparently he had been promoted and now had peon runners of his own. On any given trip they would bring upwards of 75 pounds back to be packaged and distributed for personal consumption. To better put this into perspective, imagine a typical bale of hay divided up between three backpacks. This little dance would happen two, sometimes three times a week! The only change would be a different rental car and they would take turns being the driver. Except for Willy, he was a felon and not allowed into Canada.

As Tina continued her tale, I could see the facial expression of the detective slowly change; it was Christmas in July and she knew it. Now all we needed was to prove that everything Tina was telling us was the truth. I asked her if she knew who his contact was on the other side - she didn't. I asked her if she knew where he stayed when he went up there; her first response was that she didn't know but then she remembered something critical.

"His cell phone doesn't work when he crossed into Canada. So he'd call me from the hotel." She said.

At first I wasn't convinced that this was helpful information to us until she made another confession.

"Last time he was there he called me at the house and I remember writing the number on a notepad by our phone in the basement."

"Any chance you still have that note?" I inquired, obviously more than a little hopeful.

Though she was certain the note had been destroyed, she was equally certain the same notepad still sat by the phone. Without questioning me, she contacted Luke and had him bring the notepad into the office.

Luke showed up slightly confused and we filled him in on our reason for making him fetch the pad. I saw him trying to refrain from letting his emotions take over. He knew of his wife's transgressions and seemed to be doing his best to deal with that fact, but to now realize that this was happening under his roof and in front of their other children was going to take a little more self-control. He and his wife shared a glare, which told us this was probably not the last time this topic would be discussed.

The pad was indeed blank but I had an implausible idea. I was going to attempt to use a super special undercover private investigator technique … just kidding, I actually learned this as a kid. Taking a pencil, I lightly started to shade over the entire front of the paper and *like magic* the numbers began to appear, well, all the numbers but the last; no big deal that just left me with 10 choices. Lucky for us this was a notepad which was rarely used, and now with the indents from the pen Tina used to write down his number I had my next direction.

I chatted a little longer with the detective after Luke and Tina left. I told her I needed some time to take this phone number and see what would come of it;

then I'd be sure to fill her in so she could complete their goal of making some arrests.

On the seventh try, I hit the jackpot. I pretended to be Dale and pleasantly chatted with the female desk clerk on the other end of the line. I told her that my company was being audited and that I was in dire need of all my receipts, including the phone records, from my stays at the hotel. This was during the time of Bush's reign as President and I knew the majority of Canadians were not exactly fans of his, so I decided to play upon that. I went on and on cursing the government and all the hoops they were making me jump through. I apologized to her for the inconvenience and she was more than willing to share her anti-Bush opinions! I fueled her fire, and before too long she agreed to help me with whatever I needed just to "stick it to the man." I gave her my (untraceable) fax number and within the hour had over 87 pages of receipts and records in my hands!

Dale's cell didn't work up there so I knew we had him; every name and every number of every date he was up in Canada. This was a prime example of how different our game rules are compared to that of law enforcement's. We had uncovered enough information to give officers some solid leads to go on.

We handed them a package wrapped with a big red bow; everything from a list of his many house guests in town to the details of his Canadian vacations. They had names and numbers to follow up with on both sides of the border. With this pretty package, the detectives ran their own sting operation. After watching and recording Dale's drug trafficking process, from the runner drop off to pick up, they made an arrest on the Idaho side with both in the vehicle and over 75 pounds of weed on board!

We had even dug up an IRS 1099 form from Dale's uncle's so called "company" for over $60,000. They wanted the government to think that he was being paid for his contracting expertise when, in reality, Dale would give Uncle the cash from the drug deals and he, in turn, would pay him back with a business check - naturally keeping a cut for himself. This opened even more doors for federal law enforcement; they now had just cause to investigate potential money laundering.

I waited a few days for the detective to put all her ducks in a row using the information from us and then she called me:

"We got 'em, Erin. We got them good."

Now I could make my call to our clients and set up a meeting. They were more than thrilled with the results, and for the first time I saw hope in both of their eyes. I wanted to make certain they understood that even though this was a huge point on our side, it was still in the hands of the courts and nothing there was ever a slam dunk.

Dale was all "hammered up" and had no other option but to pick a lawyer, and we couldn't have been more pleased with his choice! We do enough in the community that we are familiar with the majority of the attorneys; if not by name, at least by reputation. Dale's pick had earned the nickname in the industry as "the deal maker", which was extremely good news for our clients. He was the type of lawyer who wanted to do very little unless he knew the case was a no-brainer. Thanks to our findings it was indeed a no-brainer, but not for Dale! In less than one week Dale's slacker of an attorney called and a deal was on the table. Really? Seriously? What a "surprise"!

The law in Idaho states that if a woman gets pregnant when she is married, her husband is revered as the father - even if he is not the sperm donor. That doesn't mean the donor has no rights, it just makes it that much harder for him to get custody - especially if the marriage stays intact after the affair ends. The courts will usually lean towards the mother and her husband, but nothing is for certain in the hands of a judge so my clients needed to make sure he went away and went away for good. Our clients only wanted this one thing, so when they countered with their requirement it was not surprising that Dale didn't react well.

His immediate response was not only "no," but "hell no!" There was no way he was willingly going to give up his parental rights, so he needed a little nudge in the right direction. Luke and Tina's lawyer had a reputation in the legal community and it was a very good thing because she was known as a legal pit bull and she had Dale right where he wanted him.

"Fine, don't sign. We have enough evidence to drown you and we have no problem going that route. If you're lucky you'll be out in time to see the boy graduate from high school."

Needless to say, Dale's attorney advised Dale to take the deal.

He did, in fact, take the deal and was out of the boy's life forever! His counterparts were charged with multiple felonies. Hopefully he learned.

Dales' mommy was not pleased but was warned of what would happen to her legally if she harassed the family ever again; that was enough to shut her up. Uncle's fate is unknown as the case is still under investigation with local drug enforcement.

Our clients were elated. Our fee was minuscule compared to what a full-blown custody case could have cost them, not to mention a potentially bleak outcome.

The Rule: Don't have affairs! You will always be caught. Don't deal drugs; chances are you will end up in the State Pen as someone's new girlfriend! And the most important rule is to be forgiving, not one person is perfect. Being forgiving will have a lasting effect on the lives of all of those around you!

Tina, Luke, baby boy and the rest of the family moved out of Idaho and made a clean start in another state. They currently own and operate a successful farm. The sky is the limit for this child's future, and he is now blessed to grow up in a loving home with parents who rose above adultery to put the well-being of their children first.

Rule #6:

LEAVE NO STONE UNTURNED – THE WORM WILL EVENTUALLY CRAWL OUT

Many of our cases come from lawyers, either by referral or directly with them and their offices. Just like any industry, there are good lawyers and there are some we just shake our heads wondering how in hell did they pass the bar? These are the attorneys who motivate all of the multiple "lawyer jokes" and the negative knee-jerk reaction everyone gets at the mere mention of the word.

This case was with one of the good attorneys; he is both knowledgeable and ethical. If you want to learn what kind of attorney one is just golf with them. If a lawyer is a proficient golfer and tells you he spends more time playing than he does working and he's older or retired, it tells you he did well and is enjoying life. Well, I can tell you firsthand this young lawyer has a lot of work, because his golf game left a lot to be desired.

His client was being charged with a DUI and, naturally, the client said he didn't do it. His client told him he was not the one driving the car. It was interesting considering I've never heard that before.

Let's back up a bit and fill you in on the details. Our client was hanging out one night at a local watering hole. And by hole I mean hole, like "hole in the wall". It was the saddest excuse for a bar ever! It would have most of us too frightened to walk through the front door out of fear of catching something that took medicine to get rid of, or worse yet, catching something nothing could get rid of! It was dark and dirty with every possible holiday decoration still hanging off the walls and ceiling; from New Year's wishes in the front window, shamrock streamers lining the hallway to the bathroom, July 4th banners above the bar, pumpkin and goblins hanging in the far corner and a small dusty fake decorated fir tree sitting on a shelf. The windows should have let some of the natural light in and probably did, the last time they were cleaned. The dust and the fingerprints suggested this had been done sometime in the 1990's. Guess that saves on having to tint them. It was not a place that attracted new people.

Our client found himself there on a Wednesday night blowing off steam from a tough day at work and catching up with a pal, who just so happened to be the longtime bartender at the tavern. Ken (at least that's what you think his name is) was a decent man with a good job who, for the most part, had a habit of making good decisions. He did have a prior DUI on his record from years past and was committed to never getting into that situation again. For those who knew him, it made this recent arrest that much more suspicious.

He came in with the intent of one beer but, as intentions have a tendency to do, this one got a little off track. He was in no shape to drive and never for a moment considered getting behind the wheel. His bartender buddy suggested calling him a cab but it also wasn't an option. The distance to his house wasn't far and he could have walked home. A little bit of a jaunt and by the time he got home most of the night's efforts would be wearing off; again not an option. His main concern was getting his car home. Considering the bar's neighborhood, anyone would hesitate to leave their car in its lot. Just parking it there while you grabbed a quick beer is a risk! But it was more so with Ken's ride. He had worked hard and rewarded himself with his dream car.

It was a Chevy Camaro, the classic American man's dream car. It was a 1968 car living in the 2000's, fully restored to the original paint and condition. If all you had was a picture of this car today you'd swear it was taken back in the 60's. It had beautiful outward curving fenders with a narrower middle, similar to the other "coke bottle" cars like the Corvette and Dodge Charger. It was perfect; and not just the outside. Accompanying the shine of the gun metal grey exterior was a flawless interior, with customized upholstery to replicate it back to a time when it was first driven out of the factory. Then there was under the hood; that, too, was refurbished to mimic the intent that the auto maker had back in the late sixties. It was designed to move … fast. With close to 400 horsepower it drove unlike any other vehicle. Most of the cars today primarily focus on gas savings and limited exhaust emissions. The only thing on the minds of the engineers behind this car was to make it speedy and sexy, and they did just that! There was no way this car should spend a night anywhere but tucked away in a cozy garage. So, Ken's buddy arranged another bar patron to drive Ken home in his own car and then would have a cab pick him up at Ken's house to bring him back to the bar. Seemed simple enough and Ken wasn't going to question his friend; if he was comfortable with this guy then so was he. The two strangers left the pub and while Ken struggled to stumble in the passenger's seat, his chauffeur was more than pleased to take his seat behind the wheel! Now before we continue on it's important to explain the difference between driving this level of car compared to that of the modern day Ford Taurus. It's like Fred Flintstone's car compared to George Jetson's. If you weren't familiar with the power of a stock car then this was an extremely unique experience and not one to play around with.

Ken didn't take the time to interview the driver and get his driving resume, which was too bad. They barely made it out of the tavern's parking lot before he piled it up! That's right. He hit the gas when he got to the end of the road and rammed it straight into the fence of the business across the street! The front end hit the corner post of the chain-link fence and forced the concrete out of the ground, lifting the car and high-centered in the air. The driver gets out, leaving his semi-passed out copilot in the seat next to him and makes a beeline back to his parked car and drives away without a word to anyone.

The next thing Ken remembers is wandering outside his now not-so-cherry car and listening to the sirens getting closer and closer. The cops cuffed and threw him into the back seat, while ignoring the usual "I didn't do it" pleas coming out of his drunken mouth.

This is where his lawyer put a call into us and we set up a meeting. My first impression, which is usually pretty spot on, was one of belief. I started the questioning; questioning that I thought was fairly simple. Things like "who was he?" and "what was him name?" Unfortunately, both answers were the same, "I don't know". I asked one more question and it wasn't until he replied the same way that we knew we had our work cut out for us. All he remembered was that his buddy the bartender got someone to drive him home, that's it.

"Let me get this straight, you not only don't know who he is but you have no idea what he looks like?"

Ken nodded, then I looked at his counsel with a stare which he read perfectly.

"Do you have any idea how tall of an order this is?"

He nodded the same way because he truly did know what he was asking. So they left us with pretty much nothing to go on. We decided to send Kaleb down to the pub to talk to our only lead, the bartender. He got there and the barkeeper seemed friendly enough, until Kaleb introduced himself and handed him his business card. Then the smile faded and the bartender, oddly, knew nothing.

We called the lawyer and let him know that Kaleb came up empty handed. We suggested that he send Ken back there to ask some questions of his own; maybe he'd get a warmer reception seeing as he was one of their own. But Ken got the same cold shoulder and his so-called pal had no recollection of what he remembered. According to him, he said Ken had a few beers and when he went into the back room to change the keg, he came back to see

Ken's bar stool was empty. He said he assumed Ken went home and that was that.

This bartender wasn't telling us everything- that was pretty obvious, so Kaleb spent the next few evenings hanging around there deliberately asking questions of the patrons and leaving his card with anyone who would take it. They all knew one another and it was more than obvious the word was out, and that no one was supposed to talk. But Kaleb had made the natives restless and eventually one of them was going to slip up. People start to get nervous and things start to slip out, at least that's what we were hoping. On the fourth night, finally, we had a small breakthrough.

Rumor had it that some guy named Mark was seen chatting up at the bar with Ken and the bartender near the end of the night in question. It came out that Mark was the produce manager at a local grocery chain store, so we decided to take this speck of a clue and make a phone call. According to the store's front office clerk there was indeed a Mark as produce manager and she was kind enough to give us his full name as well as the exact times of his next few shifts on the schedule. We pulled our background check and were not surprised to see he had a long record of drunken occurrences; drunk in public, urinating in public, disorderly conduct, DUI, anything to do with abuse of alcohol. How did this guy land a job, let alone a managerial position?

I decided it was time to pay him a visit, so I got wired up and Kaleb and I headed down to the grocer.

"Hi, are you Mark, the produce manager?"

"Yes, what can I do for you?" His response was pleasant enough, assuming he thought we were just another couple of vegetable lovers looking for the perfect kumquat.

"I'd like to talk to you about an incident that happened last month with a Camaro outside a bar on the outskirts of town."

That's when the pleasantries left and he came *unglued.* His demeanor did a complete 180-degree turn and his voice deepened as his chest rose.

"I wouldn't be caught dead in any bar and I definitely wouldn't have anything to do with a stinking GM product!" He shouted.

It was an over-the-top reaction to my simple inquiry, which had both Kaleb and I thinking the same thoughts, "this is our guy," The crowd around us started to gather as Mark continued on at the same volume:

"I'm working right now and I don't have to talk to you. You're trespassing! Get out of here before I call the cops on you!"

Now I was *convinced* he was hiding something. Usually when someone starts spewing threats that hold no truth it's because they're panicking and grasping at straws. So I decided to call his bluff.

"Ok fine. I'll come back with a subpoena and you can tell your tale to a judge."

"I'm calling the cops!" he repeated his threat again as if I didn't hear him the first time.

"Knock yourself out. I'll be back and if you thought this was uncomfortable, you just wait." I handed him my card. Kaleb and I walked out, while the patrons silently watched us leave through the automatic doors.

Kaleb and I drove back to the office convinced that we had found Ken's chauffeur. Twenty minutes later my phone rang and to my surprise it was him, except this time it was my turn to give him the cold shoulder.

"What? Are *you* sending the cops after *me* now?" I gave him just enough smack talk to get the recorder going.

To my surprise, he had completely changed his tone. He started by apologizing and was justifying his behavior by blaming it on a couple of bad days.

"Then you came in accusing me and ..."

"Wait! Back the truck up. I never accused you once. I simply asked you a question. You jumped down my throat before I even got a chance to blame anyone."

"You're right. Look, I get off at 3:00, can we meet at the coffee house across the street from the store?"

I hung up the phone and went into Kaleb's office telling him our guy not only called back but it sounded like he needed to clear his conscience. It seemed we had our guy and all we had to do was get the confession recorded.

The afternoon came and Kaleb and I entered the coffee shop to find Mark and another man sitting at a table. Mark introduced him as his assistant manager and used the words "witness" to describe why he was there with him. I pulled the recorder out of my pocket and, in clear sight, hit the button and set it on the table between all of us just before I sat down.

"Oh no, I'm not doing this." Ken stated.

I could tell he was nervous but I simply told him that he had his witness and this was one of mine. He refused again so I stood up without a word, grabbed the recorder and headed towards the door.

"Wait! I just want to talk this out."

"So let's talk. Only this is on or we'll do it again with a subpoena, your choice. I just want to ask you a few questions. If you weren't involved, then this is the time to convince me." I said.

He nodded and I sat down, once again placing the recorder on the table. He started into the conversation with a laundry list of woes from an ex-wife to an unrealistic boss. Placing my hand in the air I quickly got him back on track.

"Stop, you're making this harder than it needs to be. I don't care about any of that; just tell me where you were that night."

"I'll have to look at my calendar." He said.

"Ok, now don't go off again, but have you ever been in this pub?"

And away he went - rambling on and on about being a reformed alcoholic and how he's been clean and sober for six months and would never be in a bar; blah, blah, blah. Once again, I had to raise my hand and regain control of the conversation.

Then Kaleb asked a question. “So, you’d never be caught dead in a GM, is that right?”

Mark looked at him a bit confused, so Kaleb repeated himself and reminded him of the comment he made during our first meeting in the middle of the produce department. I knew it was a set-up because after we left this morning, we took down all the license plates of the cars in the employee parking lot and had found the car that was registered in his name.

“That’s right, I hate 'em.” Mark was adamant.

“Don’t you currently drive a Geo Metro? Correct me if I’m wrong but isn’t that a GM product?” Kaleb was reeling him in.

He hung his head in silence and we were ready to seal the deal.

“I think we better take a look at that calendar of yours and hopefully you can find someone to corroborate your whereabouts that night.” I simply stated.

Mark nodded and we waited as he walked across the street to his work place to retrieve his datebook, which just so happened to be on the front seat of the afore-mentioned Geo! As he ventured back a little voice popped up in my head - he agreed to do that *a little too quickly.* Hmmmm. Now I had a little bit of doubt building. Was he so eager because he had time after we left the store to write in the book and make a few calls of his own, and this was a set-up? He came back and sat down putting the date book on the table, right in front of us, and started flipping through the pages.

"Here it is. Oh yeah, I was in the city helping a friend remodel his bathroom." Mark said with confidence.

He continued on saying he had stayed overnight because he had the next day off and was going to help him some more. Oh, oh, what was happening here? He then pulled out his phone and found his friend's number in his contacts and offered it to me without me even asking. Was this part of his plan? I had to call his bluff so I asked to see his phone and, without hesitation, he handed it over to me. While he watched I scrolled through his history, and to my dismay there were no calls in or out since we had spoken and absolutely no texts either way as well. It was almost a month ago, so having forgotten he was out of town wasn't that farfetched. I listened to him detail this weekend and there was something about his demeanor that had me believing his story. But one thing wasn't sitting well.

"So if this is the truth, why did you completely go off on me?" I asked.

"I don't know, I guess I spent most of my life being accused of things, bad things that I actually did when I was drinking. I overreacted when I thought you were doing the same. I'm so used to defending myself that I just slipped back into that mode even though I've been sober for months."

Damn it. It actually made sense to me. So with his permission I used his phone and called his remodeling pal right then in the coffee house. He was telling the truth.

Now what? Kaleb and I left there completely baffled. From the beginning we thought we had our guy and to have it dead end was not an option we thought we'd be dealing with. I made a call to the lawyer and burst his hopeful bubble. I suggested Kaleb and Ken go back and continue asking around; maybe, just maybe something would turn up. Other than that, I wasn't sure what direction to turn.

The next day I got a call from Ken's attorney and I couldn't believe what Ken found out. It seems that the manager in question was not from the local store! Same store name, but a different location! If that wasn't ironic enough, guess what this manager's name was? Yep, Mark.

Unbelievable isn't it? What are the odds of finding an ex-drunk with the same name doing the same job? Oops nobody's perfect! At least the trail was hot again, so we thought. After a phone call to the store's manager, we were told this Mark was no longer working there and, oddly enough, had quit the day after the night in question; he wasn't giving me numbers or addresses. Guess we'll have to make another trip to the grocery store.

Kaleb drove there that afternoon and starting asking some of the other employees questions, and passed around his card in case someone happened to remember anything that might be helpful. He spoke with one man in the produce department who was particularly stand-offish, with good reason, as he was one of this Mark's closest buddies. Kaleb hadn't left the building when this man put a call into Mark tattling on how a PI was snooping around asking all sorts of questions about him.

Obviously, Mark didn't appreciate people poking around in his business and, in his arrogance, made a call to the number on the card Kaleb left behind.

"What the hell are you doing? Who do you think you are?" Mark was upset.

Two very good questions Kaleb thought as he started recording the call; a bit of an attitude but Kaleb was able to play that to his own advantage.

“What can you tell me about a Camaro being parked on a chain link-fence?” Kaleb calmly asked.

That was the only fuel Kaleb needed to feed this egotistical idiot’s fire! Kaleb kept him on the phone close to a half an hour asking rhetorical questions and getting a barrage of expletives hurled back at him as answers. In this 30 minutes Mark managed to change his story three times; Kaleb had him so worked up he wasn’t sure if he was coming or going. Mark started saying that he was at the bar with his wife playing pool, and then stated that he had never been there! Kaleb asked him, "Are you telling me no one would know you there?”

Silence. Sweet guilty silence. Before he got two words out, Kaleb cut him off mid-sentence and left him with a little more to think about.

“I think we’ve got our guy and I think you’re him.” Click. (Whoa, good job Kaleb….)

Meanwhile, I’m picking apart the police investigation, or *lack thereof* as it was in this case. They took no fingerprints, canvassed no neighbors and didn’t even bother to walk into the bar to ask if anyone saw anything! They simply saw a drunk man wandering outside his smashed-up car and hauled him in guilty without question, discarding *anything* he was trying to tell them!

The attorney called and was ready to throw his hands up in defeat, especially after our miss with the first Mark. I convinced him to give us a bit more time. I didn't fill him in on the *new* Mark because this time I wanted to be certain before getting anyone's hopes up. I convinced him to put off Ken's hearing one more time and let us finish the leads we had.

Shortly after I hung up with him, Kaleb came in my office and filled me in on his latest events. We were back in business and this time we just may have found what we needed to prove Ken's innocence. As Kaleb and I compared notes his cell phone rang and the smile on his face told me exactly who was on the other line. He let it ring a few more times, set it to record, and put it on speaker as he set it on my desk.

"Hello." Kaleb is calm.

"You hung up before I finished, you SOB!"

CLICK. I just smiled because Kaleb was playing a mind game I had taught him, and playing it quite well, if I do say so myself.

Within minutes it rang again and I was anxious to see what step Kaleb would take next. He once again let it ring multiple times then he answered it with authority.

"Unless you are ready to cut through this BS and tell me the truth, quit bothering me."

Not what the caller expected, and we could tell by the silence that Kaleb caught him way off guard.

"My wife will testify for me…"

"No doubt," Kaleb cut him off. "You've had plenty of time to plan that."

"You can ask anyone, a lot of people there know me."

It was time for Kaleb to pull out the big guns, even if it was a stretch of the truth.

"We're currently pulling the fingerprints off the steering wheel as we speak and they're going to match yours, aren't they?"

Complete silence again. And what came out of his mouth next was the nail in his proverbial coffin.

"Ask anyone, ask my brother-in-law. He's the bartender there."

BAMM! Now it all makes sense, that's why no one was talking! That's why no one knew anything; it was a family affair.

With two simple words Kaleb once again hung up on his caller, "Thank you."

Kaleb could not wait to head back down to the bar and re-question the bartender, the same man that had nothing to contribute the multiple times Kaleb was in there. Catching someone in a lie and being able to rub their faces in it was an occasion neither of us ever pass on. Only this time, when Kaleb entered the dark dreary door of the pub he was met by an unfriendly barkeeper. He was pissed and went off on Kaleb the minute he saw him. Then he kicked him out of the bar. This only reinforced his guilt so Kaleb simply smiled and left, but he was not done.

That night, before the bar closed, Kaleb headed back there and parked outside in the lot and waited. We knew from our previous investigating the bartender lived close enough to walk, and did so because he was without a license. Kaleb knew he would have to come out and when he did he'd ask the questions he wanted to ask earlier.

Within the hour Kaleb caught sight of the man's familiar physique as it left the darkened pub. Slowly, still staying in his car, he pulled up beside the walker and rolled down his window just enough so he could be heard.

"It's called perjury."

The walker said nothing at first and only walked faster as Kaleb patiently escorted him home.

“I told you, I don’t know anything.”

“So when I take this recording of you and compare it to the 911 call that night, are you telling me the voices won’t match?”

There was a bombshell he wasn’t expecting. Another fact that came to light during our exploring was that the call came in from the pay phone at the bar. Kaleb didn’t know until right now who actually made the call but his mannerisms told the truth. He responded with a one finger wave. Kaleb smiled back at him and slowly drove away. He had done what he came to do and knew, without a doubt, that he had successfully gotten under the bartender’s skin.

The next morning I came into the office and we had three messages all from the same number. It was Mark’s dear old dad who decided to chime in on the situation. The calls came late at night and by the threatening slurs I guessed it was a little after happy hour. Seemed the family came from a long line of drunken fools and we were listening to the leader of the clan. As if that wasn’t enough, he called back around noon and apparently his happy hour lasted a lot longer than 60 minutes. He was still hammered, so I let him ramble on as I recorded every word. He was getting a lawyer, going to sue me and take everything I have, and asked if I knew who I was messing with. I really didn't but what I did know was that Daddy Dearest just gave us confirmation that this time we definitely had the right guy.

We hadn't met Mark face to face or his father; we just spoke to them over the phone. But these calls had sealed the fate for our client Ken. We put all our findings together and gave it to the attorney who, in turn, called the prosecutor.

"Your case has too many holes," he told her. "I want to see proof like fingerprints on the steering wheel or witnesses, anything the police have."

We knew that wasn't possible considering the lack of attention for detail on the part of the officers. But, we suggested that Ken's attorney first ask the prosecutor for this just to drive home these same facts in her mind and before he shared our findings. She agreed and when the cops told her exactly what we already knew he filled her in on all the other details pointing the finger at the actual guilty driver. He shared the many phone calls and visits that we had recorded over the last month with Mark, the bartender, and even Daddy. Now it was her turn to be silent.

Less than a week went by when Ken's attorney got the call. The case was dropped and all charges were dismissed!

The Rule: A case is not airtight unless it is the truth. If it's not the truth eventually it sinks like a submarine! In this part of the country it never surprises me who is related to who. If you run into a brick wall working a case start looking at who the uncles, brothers cousin is, and you will find their related to the case! Or a Congressman or both, either way your job just got harder.

So now you're probably wondering about the others, the guilty parties. Unfortunately, they got away with it.

I know. It doesn't sit well with me either, but there's the bigger picture. Our mission was to prove the innocence of our client and we did that. The rest of them will reach their destiny in time; at least that's what I tell myself. I suggest you do the same; it lessens the pain.

Rule #7:

ALWAYS USE TECHNOLOGY TO YOUR ADVANTAGE

Idaho is assumed to be racist by the majority of the other states in the country; thanks to some of our unpopular, idiotic, radical, *ex*-residents. The Aryan Nations is a white-supremacist group that was unfortunately headquartered in northern Idaho from 1970 until 2001. Even though they've been gone over ten years their stench still smells strong when anyone mentions Idaho. That or potatoes, which if you ask anyone that lives here they'd gladly take vegetables over bigotry.

This fact alone is the reason why this case got so blown out of proportion. Our state is a little touchy when it comes to racial issues, even though that's not necessarily exactly what this case was.

Six high school students were best buds for the last three-plus years and hung out all the time. Like typical boys they harassed each other, and labeled each other with the most unappealing nicknames they could come up with. They consistently insulted and ragged on each other the way girls hugged and giggled. One of them drove a beat-up old Toyota truck and seeing as two others had full size pickups, they called him "Toy Boy" with his want-to-be pickup. Another was a football star and was in pretty good shape during the season. When it ended and he stopped the training his junk food habit caught up with him quickly and he was packing around a noticeable amount of belly fat; he was Fat Boy Slim, which shortened to Slim amongst the group. Then there was Dune Coon. By looking at Alan you wouldn't necessarily be able to pin-point his heritage. His skin was slightly darker than the rest of the gang but nothing that made him stand apart. What did stand him apart was his mother. She was Islamic and his dad was American, hence his nickname. It was healthy ribbing and they each dealt it out equally and consistently.

The latest gag was on Slim. Usually one of the five came up with the idea and the others joined in on the gag. The leader switched depending on who had the thought. But regardless, the remaining four would follow along and contribute anyway they could just to be involved. Coon headed up this one and decided to target Slim. Slim had his sights on Jessica. Jessica was a well-developed junior that got the attention of all the boys in school, but for whatever reason she was looking back at Slim. Her best friend's younger sister told Toy Boy's sister that Slim liked her and it got back to Jessica. She told her best friends sister to tell Toy Boy's sister to tell Toy Boy to tell Slim that she'll meet him at his locker Friday after 3rd period (or something simple like that). However it happened, all pals were well aware that Slim was anxious for his meeting. Coon decided this was the perfect time to prank him. The bell rang and as Slim waited by his locker the others were watching inconspicuously from around the corner. Jessica showed up and they started chatting. Things were looking pretty good for their boy until he reached for the latch on his locker. With one pull the door flew open and over forty cans of Slim Fast diet shakes rolled onto the floor and down the hallway.

The uncontrollable laughter from around the corner brick walls told Slim all he needed to know. So, in his mind it was game on and the other 5 knew this wasn't the end. This was the pattern they had for over three years, so payback was not only expected but encouraged.

A few weeks passed and it wasn't until Coon got his new truck that an idea came to Slim. If the topic of conversation among the boys wasn't sports or girls it was definitely about trucks. Coon worked as a dishwasher at a fancy restaurant in town and was saving for accessories for his new ride. It was a lifted older GMC ½ ton painted army green with lower end chrome wheels. It wasn't exactly sexy, but to Coon and his pals it had the potential to be cherry and that's what counted. He got it in late November which in Idaho means we've been knee deep in winter for close to two months already. Regardless of the temperature, he had to take his friends for a cruise and with three in the cab and three huddled in the box off they went downtown. The ride was short due to the weather and the fact that Coon was scheduled to work that night at the restaurant. This is when the prank took place.

Slim, along with the four others, waited until Coon was an hour into his long shift and headed to a gas station down the road from his work. They all chipped in and bought twelve tubes of sand that Idahoans typically need to keep their vehicles on the icy roads. This was over 600 pounds of sand and it took them two vehicles to haul it to Coon's new truck. Now the fun started. One by one they cut open and emptied the sand into the bed of Coon's truck. Then they strategically placed over a dozen GI Joe figurines on the mound. Some they had doctored up with a black marker coloring their faces and sports tape wrapped around the heads as mock turbans. There were even a few of these with their heads cut off and laying in the sand. The coup de grâce was the sign made out of cardboard and a paint stir stick shoved into the middle of this giant pile of sand. The five of them quickly finished their handy work and anxiously waited for Coon to finish his shift.

It was a long and brutal night at his job. The restaurant was crazy busy and his manager was in a mood and since poop travels downhill, Coon took the brunt of it. He walked through the brightly lit carport to find his newly decorated truck. On any other given night this might have gotten the reaction it was intended to, but not tonight. Matter-of-fact it had the opposite reaction. He stopped and stared at the drawn cartoon camel and read aloud the words written in black marker "#1 DUNE COON - FU Fatty!"

There was no time to gather his thoughts as he punched in the familiar numbers on his cell phone. He didn't have to think about which pal it was considering who he pranked last, which made his response that much more confusing for the person answering the ring.

"You $ ***er &***er! I'm going to kick your ass!"

Slim was waiting for the call and was ready to flip crap back like they always did.

"Yeah right, like you could ever do that!" He giggled through the phone only there was no laughing coming back.

“Who the *^%& do you think you’re screwing with? You think this is funny?”

In all honesty Slim really did think it was funny-they all did. Normally Coon would have too. It was now that Slim realized that his hoax victim was not taking it the way it was meant.

“It was a joke! Relax. You know like the crap you pulled on me at the lockers?”

“This is not a joke. Meet me at Super One parking lot at midnight and I’ll show you how funny this isn’t!”

“You serious?” Slim’s patience was wearing thin considering his pal’s over-the-top response.

“Yeah. Show up and see when I kick the s#!t out of you!”

“You kick the s#*t out of me? Right, like that’s going to happen. Fine, I’ll see you at midnight.”

They both hung up at the same time but couldn’t have been on two opposite pages. Coon was ready to battle and Slim was planning on settling his friend down in person. This happened in the heat of the Gulf War which would have easily explained anyone’s reaction. But this circumstance was nothing like what it looked like from the outside.

This was a practical joke played among friends, nothing more.

Slim was in the parking lot a few minutes early and sat waiting in his dad's white Ford pickup truck. He was listening to the tunes, not really concerned about what was to come. It was his friend for crying out loud, he'd get here and they'd talk it out and move on. End of story. If he thought it would amount to anything else he would never have come alone.

He recognized the truck pulling in off the main street and gave himself a little chuckle as he saw sand blowing out the back. Coon parked with his headlights beaming on Dad's passenger door. Slim reached for the door handle anticipating Coon would do the same. He anticipated wrong and froze as he was blinded by five additional sets of headlights speeding towards him. One by one they deliberately parked circling around the Ford, pinning him in like it's the Wild Wild West. Jumping back in behind the wheel he squints through the beaming light and he could make out more than one head in a few of the cars.

Now he was starting to worry. He wasn't a small guy and rarely walked away from a fight as the loser. One on one - no problem. Two on one? Maybe. But six or more to one? Not likely. Panic started to set in and Slim realized that talking it out wasn't an option tonight. He could stay there locked in the vehicle, but the whooping he'd get from his dad for bringing home his fancy truck all beat up would be worse than the one he was facing now. Without much thought, he reached into the console and felt around for something he hoped his dad still kept there. Pulling his right hand out of the console he slowly lowered the passenger window with his left. Lifting and straightening his right hand he pointed a red laser beam through the windshield and held the dot steady on his so-called friend's chest.

It was unmistakable to all what had transpired and it was a definite game changer for Coon and his recruited posse. No words were needed. As infuriated as Coon was, he was at least alert enough to realize the severity of the situation. Putting the sand filled truck in reverse, he slammed the gas pedal to the floor and watched the Ford move just as fast forward as he had just moved backward. Six to one are good odds unless the one is holding a stainless steel Kember semi-automatic .45 caliber Model Pro Carry handgun with handle-activated laser sight.

Slim didn't step off the gas until his dad's truck was back in the garage and the door was safely closed behind him. It wasn't until now that he realized he still had the firearm tightly gripped in his right hand. Slowly he returned it back to its spot in the console and went into the house to sleep off the night's strange and unpredicted ending. He didn't get much sleep.

Within the hour Slim's dad was awakened by a consistent knocking and ringing of his doorbell. Swinging the door open in anger he was taken aback when he came face to face with two uniformed officers. Still half asleep, he tried to wrap his head around what the policeman were attempting to tell him. Slim came out per his dad's request and both of them woke up quickly when they began reading his son his rights. The rest of the early morning was a blur to both father and son. They cuffed him, led him out of the house and into the back seat of the police car. It wasn't until hours later that Slim and his dad got the details behind the early morning arrest. He was being charged for Malicious Harassment, otherwise known as a hate crime, and Aggravated Assault with a Deadly Weapon.

It seemed that Coon was not happy with the loss at the parking lot. So he placed a 911 call claiming a kid from school had been harassing him and then vandalized his new truck. He had told the officers they planned to "work it out" on their own in the parking lot but Slim showed up with a gun and threatened to kill him and his three friends, who just so happened to be with him.

Slim's parents hired a lawyer and the lawyer's first call was to us.

This was going to be a tricky one as it was a classic "he said, he said" kind of case. The encouraging news was that it involved minors. Encouraging because I was confident that if we dug deep enough someone or ones would slip up and the truth would eventually come out. We just had a lot of work ahead of us.

My first meeting with Slim happened at the jail and I was accompanied by Dad and Mom. Unfortunately Dad and Mom were divorced so they spent the beginning of the meeting snapping back at each other flinging blame. This wasn't going to help anybody so I held both hands up- one facing each of them.

"That's enough! You have nothing to do with this other than you're his parents. So I'm going to deal with your son only. Just sit there quietly and don't talk unless I ask you a question. Got it?!"

They got the point and thankfully did as I asked. Now I could focus on Slim. I had the basic gist of the case from the attorney and from everything I'd heard it seemed to me the intent was a practical joke that went badly off course. But I wasn't leaning one way or another, I couldn't. My job was to find out who was telling the truth and for that I needed facts.

I'd been involved in hate crime cases before but this one was different. The original crime didn't match the severity of typical harassment offenses. If someone is perpetrating a hate crime they would use spray paint or keys on your car, not shaving cream. The sand dumped in the back was no more harmful than shaving cream.

"Tell me what happened."

My plan was to rake this kid over the coals and try to poke holes in his story. He didn't sway a bit from his original statement. That's usually a good sign but I wasn't giving in that easily.

"What about the sign? That was a pretty big racial slur."

He didn't even flinch and explained how Coon always said how much he hated the Muslim extremists and always referred to them as "towel heads."

"That's why we did what we did with the GI Joe's; we thought he'd get a kick out of it."

That made sense to me so I continued on with the questioning and asked about desecrating his new truck, especially since he knew how nuts he was about it.

"It was just sand. We even planned helping him clean it out the next day. A shovel and hose would take care of it."

True, it really wasn't that big of a deal. I fired more digs his way and he always had a reasonable response and explanation. This went on for nearly two hours and when we were through I "un-gagged" the parents and I left. I called his attorney and told him I believed the kid and I thought it best we interviewed the others; the four original pals and the parking lot gang. He agreed. (See? I told you he was brilliant).

We started with the pals who helped out in the prank. I spoke with each of them separately and there were a few slight differences but the overall general picture was identical. We worry when the individual accounts are too equal as they appear to have collaborated. In this case I knew they hadn't since Slim had been in jail the whole time.

Next, Kaleb and I went over to a house where we were told the parking lot kids hung out after school. Sure enough, four of the six were there and one other kid who wasn't. I introduced ourselves and told them we just wanted to talk to them about the "shooting". I exaggerated on purpose hoping the drama would entice them; it did and they welcomed us in. Naturally, I was wired just in case something useful came up, and it did.

"So what the heck happened that night? Weren't these two guys pals?" I asked.

They were all anxious to tell their account of the evening. One would barely get a thought out before someone would interrupt him with corrections. They started arguing with one another trying to prove they were the one who knew the real story. Even the kid that wasn't there had an opinion.

"So you all talk about this at school?" I was asking knowing this was a big legal no-no.

"Hell yeah, this is all anyone is talking about," bragged the odd man out, as the rest nodded in agreement.

After listening to them bicker one thing became apparent- no one there had any idea what the real story was since we had numerous different recollections. We left with a fantastic recording and now all we needed to do was speak with Alan (aka Coon). Unfortunately, word about PI's snooping around and asking questions got back to him and he was refusing to see us. So we needed another way to get him to "talk."

The very definition of "talk" is to express something by speaking; to speak; express something using speech. It wasn't that long ago this was our primary form of communication. We talk to one another in person and over the phone; both forms of communication involving speaking out loud. Fast forward a few short decades and now the word talk is almost unrecognizable. We've invaded the communication era with the use of technology. Before computers our highest accomplishment in the personal technology field was the conversion of 8 tracks to cassettes; we could now find, pause, play, eject, record and copy. Whoohoo! That was some high tech stuff. It's hard to believe most high school kids today aren't even really certain what a cassette is, and forget asking them about 8 tracks!

Talking today is not what talking was. Sure we're always in touch with one another. We overuse social media sites like Facebook and MySpace, Twitter and texting, as well as email. It's progressed from computers that filled an entire room to ones that barely fill our pockets; from multiple phone lines in our homes to none. Pay phones and pagers are a thing of the past and now our kids are plugged in before they learn to run.

It should be a world of maximum communication. Ironically these advancements have somehow made us communicate less. It has no doubt progressed our business world into realms we could only have imagined; advancements that have improved our way of working. It used to be the only one who typed in an office was the secretary. Now that's all everyone does. Each desk comes with a computer, and a laptop is mandatory when traveling on a business trip. We share documents, assemble reports, and give presentations with them. Frankly we'd be lost in business without computers. Businesses are born on websites and managed via online transactions. Businesses depend on these technologies to survive and without them these days the wheels of commerce would quickly grind to a halt. Yet, this very invention that was intended to make our business lives easier ended up making them more complex (ever lost a document or sweated over a blue screen?).

What about our personal lives? Can we actually say that technology has improved our relationships? Sure virtual shopping online is more convenient but unfortunately it's been at the cost of the actual stores making any profitable margins. Technically, we can now do a lot of our work from home so we can spend time with our families, but are we really doing that with our time away from work? When's the last time you and your family sat down at a table for dinner without a phone, headset, iPod, or notepad in hand? When was the last time you all sat down for dinner, period? And Thanksgiving doesn't count. We've raised children who no longer make eye contact when actually speaking to adults and the saddest thing about this is they don't see anything wrong with it. Their thumbs house their strongest muscle and if there's a twelve year old without his or her own cell phone then it's guaranteed that they're the oddballs. Among their friends they are constantly mocked. People share more about their thoughts and beliefs with strangers on line than they do in person with family members. These advancements in communication have somehow made us communicate less. Whew! Okay, I'm officially off my soapbox (for now).

Regardless of what side of the (wireless) line you stand on, the fact is technology is a big part of how we live our lives today and we are going to use it to our advantage. Not only does every teenager come equipped with a phone but they also have at least one social media site. So if Alan wasn't willing to talk to us in person maybe he'd talk to a "friend" of ours. What do most teenage boys like? Fast cars, tough trucks, 4-wheeling, loud music, guns, hunting, video games, sports, and zombies? Maybe... But we knew that there was something almost no teenage boy can resist- *girls.* Enter "Roxanne."

This was her opening statement on her social media page:

"I was looking for some new friends in the area and saw your profile and some of your friend's profiles and you all seem really exciting. so how often do you guys go 4 wheeling? I have a 92 Toyota that we take wheeling all the time. so tell me about yourself?"

To which Alan quickly responded:

"that's bad ass, we wheel all the time! LOL just tonight I was up playing in the snow and my starter quit on me and we towed it back to my pal's house but left it in park, pretty sure it sheared the parking pin oops. that's going to be spendy. anyways I'm 18 and born here and I wheel my 84 all day long. maybe we should meet up somewhere and you can bring your 92 wheeling with me. let me know."

We were so fortunate to *find* a girl that just so happened to have all the same things in common that Alan did! ☺ And, according to her profile picture she was so much more than pretty- she was a knockout. She had gorgeous long brunette hair with big baby blue eyes and was aspiring to be a swimsuit model or an actress. With her voluptuous figure she didn't fit the mold of the typical anorexic runway model but lingerie and swimsuits would be a perfect fit for her. With a click of a few keystrokes "Roxanne" and Coon/Alan were fast friends. They chatted everyday, sometimes for hours on end, and she would always update him with her newest pictures from her modeling portfolio. She lived in the nearby city which unfortunately (or fortunately) made it hard for them to ever meet in person but that didn't stop Alan from trying. Sadly something always got in their way and plans were canceled. The latest reason being "Roxanne" had to take her cousin to see her mom in the hospital. On the way her cousin's car broke down and her mom went to the ER in an ambulance with some severe chest pains. It turned out to be nothing more than an anxiety attack but it was pretty scary for both of them. Alan couldn't argue with this reason.

They chatted every day for almost three weeks and each day they found more things in common than just 4-wheeling. Go figure- what are the odds? "Roxanne" also loved football and was the only girl Alan knew that not only watched the games but knew the rules better than most of his guy friends. Alan's favorite NFL team was the NY Giants and (ironically) "Roxanne's" favorite team was his rival the NY Jets. You can imagine their discussions on this and her passion for sports only made him dig her that much more.

The back and forth correspondence was often and diverse. “Roxanne” just turned 21 and the fact she legally could get beer made her even more interesting to Coon and his friends, just in case her numerous half-naked pictures didn’t do the trick. They talked about trucks a lot of the time and how cool it was that they shared the same taste in music. They even think they went to the same LMFAO concert this past summer and both ended up on the floor in front of the stage. Their connection was undeniable and as teenagers tend to do nowadays, they started flirting to the point they both knew where their first actual face to face meeting would end up- which we knew couldn’t physically happen. We couldn’t afford him to find this out and waste all our efforts to this point so we had to amp things up.

It was time to reel in the fish and hopefully this long cast would pay off. Alan logged on every night as he had in the weeks past, always anxious to hook up with his new friend. Only, this time he was surprised to see that she had nothing added to her page for him. They had exchanged cell numbers but she never answered when he tried calling in the past and this time was no different. He once again got her voicemail- whose voice just so happened, oddly enough, to sound exactly the same as our office manager's!

He kept calling and checking his computer but nothing happened that night. He was starting to worry and even debated calling up his buddies and driving into the city but he was unsure of her exact address. It was after midnight the next night when the ping woke him up. He was pleased to see that it was his "Roxanne".

He immediately typed:

"where you been? I was worried. u ok?"

"Roxanne": "yeah sorry. I needed to take a break from this shitty city so my bff and I took off for the night and completely unplugged."

Alan: "what happened?"

"Roxanne": "well my bff is black, sort of, her dad is but her mom is white. We were out with some people we didn't know too well and they started making some pretty crappy racial slurs at her, we both just got fed up and then decided to clock out for the rest of the night and hung out at her place by ourselves. Don't be mad."

Alan: 'I'm not mad, matter of fact I know firsthand about that kinda s!#t."

“Roxanne”: “really? how?”

Alan: “I’m biracial. My parents are mixed too and I get flack all the time. My friends are good with it and we rib each other which is cool but I had one guy who was a real jerk and ended up pulling a gun on me.”

“Roxanne”: “omg a gun! are you ok, what happened?”

Here we go!

Alan: “yeah this kid f#@!#’d with my truck while I was working so I met him at a parking lot to beat his ass and he knew id beat his ass so he hid and came out in his dads car and pulled a gun on me then we tried to ram him before he could shoot then he peeled out and drove away before we could hit him.”

“Roxanne”: “weren’t you scared? what if he shot you?!”

Alan: “wow everyone asks that same question…well to tell you the truth not really, I’m not trying to act like a badass but I really wasn’t scared. It's not the first time I had a gun pulled on me.”

“Roxanne”: “really? so what happened is that the end of it what happened to him?”

Alan: “well I was fed up with his s!#t so I called the cops on him and he got arrested. The state is charging him with aggravated assault and malicious harassment. I have papers that I have to fill out about the whole thing and I pretty much have to decide whether or not to send him to jail. Everybody says to lock his ass up but we used to be good friends and if I do send him to jail I f#@!$’d up his whole future and I don’t know if I can do that to him.”

“Roxanne”: “well what do you think you should do?”

Alan: “I dunno I don’t wanna f#@* with his life, well anyways…what would you do?”

“Roxanne”: “wow tough one. I guess it would depend how good of friends you were and if he really meant to be such an ass. I guess I would probably just drop it and move on, no point in ruining each other’s lives at such a young age if no harm was done. If you think it may bother you or you might regret it. I’m also one of those people that doesn’t want to judge someone for the mistakes they made cuz I’m not perfect either, I don’t know who is. If the tables were turned is how you should look at it, would he do this to you? would you want your life to be ruined by a mistake you made with a friend? it seems you hold the power of someone's life in your hands, whoa that's big!"

Alan: "yeah ur right and I think I'm going to recommend the charges be dropped cuz I can't do that to my pal specially since it was meant to be joke. we pull that crap all the time on each other guess I over reacted a bit. S#@! happens."

"Roxanne": "I gotta go meet my bff ill check my messages later p.s. you seem sweet. ttyl"

With that "Roxanne" logged off and we had our fish; hook, line, and sunk! Alan had no problem opening up his soul to a complete stranger, someone he had never even seen. Social media worked to our advantage in this situation and it usually does, that's the good news. The other side is of course the bad news; our kids volunteer to open their lives to strangers. Anyone can log on and be who and whatever they want to be which is harmless until someone believes them. Intimate pictures and in-depth details of where we live, who we hang out with, when we're on vacation, and where we are at that exact time. People share things that used to be reserved for the people in our lives that have earned and deserve this kind of cherished information. Yet there it is in the hands of everyone to do with whatever thcy want. It was created to help us get closer and it definitely has done this but is it people we want close to us or our children? Sometimes... lots of times the answer is absolutely not. Keep this in mind the next time you or your kids reveal yourself to the world because there are plenty of takers out there and they are much more harmful than “Roxanne"!

We gathered the interview transcripts along with the detailed written relationship between Alan and “Roxanne” and headed over to visit with the prosecutor. This was now a losing case for Coon and the prosecutor knew this too. She had nothing left to do but throw her hands up in the air and surrender. They had no alternative but to drop the malicious harassment/ the hate crime charges. It was more than apparent this was not the intent and it truly was just a prank gone extremely awry. Regardless, she was not pleased and made a last ditch attempt to tear down the case we had built.

“I need to hear these interviews not just read the transcripts. How do I know you didn’t coerce those kids to say what you needed to hear using verbal intimidation?”

I knew she would be desperate and was half expecting this type of response, so I had a flash drive ready to go in my pocket.

“I think you’ll find everything you need on there. I made it specifically for you so you can keep it.”

This was not what she expected and there's nothing I like better than to watch the sails of an arrogant lawyer slowly crash to the bottom of the boat without a breeze in sight.

Slim's attorney was gifted and more than capable of taking our facts and turning them into a winning case for his client. He was able to prove without a doubt he was using the gun in self-defense and wanted the charges of assault with a deadly weapon also dropped. Even though this was the case, the fact remains it was still a teenager with a gun. They reduced the charge to brandishing (to wave or flaunt a weapon menacingly).

Let me help explain this charge a little better. Basically you can legally carry a gun with a concealed weapons permit but you just can't show it off. I remember a trip I took to Montana for a case and I drove over one night after work. It was in the middle of winter and I stopped for coffee at a dive of a gas station in the middle of nowhere- not unusual in Montana. Wanting to keep the truck warm I left it running but locked the doors.

Upon exiting the store I see three drunken cowboys lounging by my pickup. They saw me looking at them and I quickly threw down my coffee. I knew full well they were looking to do more than say "hi." I deliberately took my right hand and reached it behind my back holding it there underneath my jacket. They were drunk but not so drunk they didn't recognize the international signal of "don't be stupid – I have a gun!" They moved away from the truck and I got in and drove away. No one had to know my gun was actually locked in the console of the running truck the whole time. This was not brandishing. Brandishing would be if I actually had my gun on me, pulled it out from behind my back, and unashamedly flashed it in their direction. Not pointing it at them, simply explaining to them that I had a friend and that it's best for everyone that they move away from my vehicle.

If an idiot cuts you off on the highway and you drive by him with your switchblade knife held up against your window, that's brandishing. Yelling and screaming with one finger held up against the same window is not brandishing. Anyway, I think you get the point. Bottom line is it was nothing compared to the original charges so they gladly accepted the alternative. Slim was released with all other charges dropped.

The Rule: Boys will be boys! Life is too short to try to come up with laws that cover every possible stupid act. Let's just have one that covers them all. It would be: "I had head up my butt misdemeanor."

Witnessed by their four mutual friends Slim went to a much deserved cuff-to-fists with Coon and just like that the gang was once again back together. I'd like to say the pranks stopped but boys will be boys. They just learned to take it a little bit better.

And, unfortunately "Roxanne" got a job out of state and had to leave before they had a chance to hook up. For Alan's sake, she thought it best that they no longer kept in touch.

Rule #8:

GO WITH YOUR GUT REGARDING POTENTIAL CLIENTS

Every once in a while a client comes our way and everything in our being tells us that this case is better left alone. This was that client.

It's a typical day and the phone rings with a potential client on the other end... she wanted to come down right away and wanted directions. She was told it was best to make an appointment and we could send her the appropriate paperwork to fill out first. She was adamant about seeing someone today and wouldn't take any other answer. I overheard the conversation from down the hallway so signaled the receptionist to transfer it to me.

The woman's voice was frantic and she was speaking loud and fast. She started with claims of fraud and needed my help to get the man that was doing this to her, even though I wasn't sure what *this* was yet. Apparently she was the bookkeeper for a company called Friends United Network, or FUN for short, and she hadn't received her pay check in over 3 months. She continued on and described the company in detail and I felt the need to cut her off before she got too deep.

"What is it exactly you want us to do for you?" I asked, hoping it would shorten the conversation. It didn't.

She continued on and I caught only small pieces of the rambling, something about needing to take care of her cats and without this money they would starve. I waited until her next long inhalation and interrupted once again telling her to please just send us the information and we'd look at it. I told her there may not be too much we could do for her but I would look at the documents and let her know.

We hung up and I came out to the front office where everyone was waiting to hear the details.

"There's something off with this one." I said. I knew this for sure. "Let's see if she sends in the information and I'll take a look like I promised."

Well, she did indeed send us information. I opened it and read through only part of it and I instantly knew what this so-called organization was all about.

Friends United Network (or FUN) was a pyramid scheme that promised wealth and personal satisfaction beyond your imagination. Their primary hook was members were helping the world be a better place and it even said they had a strong interest in animal rescue programs. They used fancy words to manipulate people into thinking they were doing good and being rewarded financially for their kindness.

Below is actual wording taking directly off of their "Overview Summary" and you can see for yourself the kind of garbage they were attempting to sell:

INTRODUCTION:

- FUN is a humanitarian organization that has spent years of researching and developing methods and plans to help our earth and all the people on it. Basically, we've been a "think tank" for six of our seven years of existence.

- FUN consists of a network of individuals, ranging from aerospace engineers and project managers to legal and financial consultants to marketing professionals and computer wizards, who are all dedicated to start a purifying system that helps solve the many problems we have, such as poverty, poor health, and our environmental problems, to name a few.

- FUN's aim is to create a very large database of people in need who enjoy being rewarded for helping others in need. The same database will also be utilized to help create the solutions we need.

SCOPE: To implement the beginning of a new way to help mankind and its environment.

PURPOSE: To help eliminate general financial dissatisfaction in order to reduce crime and wars, to help enhance the health of our earth and its people."

And the B.S. kept on going for over 6 pages and ended with the ultimate load of crap.

SUMMARY:

- FUN has designed several concepts, each capable of generating billions per year to help outside charities, as well as our own half-way housing for the homeless of all ages.

- They will be shown a better way of life, which is the FUN way toward self-esteem, the American way and a quality of life for themselves and their heirs.

- FUN will continue to use their hearts and minds to develop solutions that avoid poverty, crime, terrorism, dissatisfaction, global warming, toxic waste, energy savings, just to mention a few."

They made sure they hit every possible charity and cause as to be certain and pull on each and every heart string, from poverty and war, to global warming and animal rescue. They only thing more unbelievable than the crap being flung around on ink was the fact that many, and I mean many, many people fell for it. The next part of this member package consisted of 20 more pages of crud detailing the various *lists* that you could get your name on- of course depending how much you wanted your initial investment to be. The range started at $1,000 and believe it or not, went up to $100,000; and people were buying in, lots of people!

This is how members were told it would work. Members are encouraged to donate a significant amount to which ½ of their donation would go directly to the cause of their choice per the ample list provided by FUN. However, you would give the total amount to FUN and they would donate it on your behalf (right!). Then, the second half of your donation would secure you a spot on the list they called the "Knights of the Round Table Champions". A portion of every additional person's donation goes to the person who currently held the top spot on this list. When this person reached their financial payoff (an amount that was pre-determined by the buy-in amount), they would fall off and the next person in line would begin to receive their financial rewards. This would continue on so everyone who contributed would eventually hold the top spot and be rewarded with millions of promised dollars. The paperwork detailed the financial equations of how the system worked. Again it looked good on paper but realistically it truly fell into the "too good to be true" category.

The more I read further into this stack of papers, the more I was convinced that it was one-hundred percent a scam. Then I got closer to the end where the so-called legalities were. I couldn't help but notice the same name show up time and time again. Richard Byrne. There it was in very small black print: "The sole signature will be Richard Byrne, CEO of Friends United Network." First, I think the word they were looking for was "signatory", but I'm not surprised it wasn't spell-checked. Secondly, who reads this garbage and still runs to get their check book out? Can you say Ponzi?

I read enough to know it was a major scam but still wasn't convinced that there was anything we could do for her. I decided to put it aside and look at it later on, when I had more of a chance. I never got that chance because she decided to pop in on her own later that same week.

Our offices are in the corner of an L-shaped building that also houses other businesses. There is a main glass door that opens into a foyer that we share with an accounting firm; you turn left for them and right for us. When you first walk into our front door you're standing in the lobby with a few chairs on the left and the main desk on the right. Above this main desk are two monitors for our surveillance cameras. One is aimed at the foyer and the other just outside in the parking lot. You venture down a hallway with the bathroom to the left and two offices on the right. The end of the hallway has a right turn and three bigger offices are at that end. My office was around this corner and on the right. I couldn't see the lobby from the desk but I could hear things. I also had two monitors hung in the corner; one showing the foyer and the other the lobby.

It has become instinctual when the front door chime rings, I automatically look up- like Pavlov's dog. This particular day, when I reacted I ended up staring at the screen not exactly certain what I was looking at. I waited for a bit and heard the front desk receptionist, "Todd", ask if she had an appointment and she did not. I noticed Todd slowly started to roll backwards on the office chair as if he was trying to get away from her. This was odd enough that I decided to go upfront and see if I could help.

The first thing that hit me was the odor, but I'll get to that later. Standing in the lobby was a woman in her late 50's or so. She was wearing a knee length bright yellow raincoat yet it hadn't rained here in months. Accompanying this jacket was a pair of winter boots but snow wasn't due for months. She had her jeans tucked into these boots. Her most unusual accessory of all was her hat. The smell took precedent, so the hat became a vague oddity in the corner of my mind as I really needed to address the smell that was permeating the foyer. With eyes burning and throat closing I suggested we step outside and talk. The door wasn't even closed behind us before I heard the windows inside fly open and the over-misting of the bathroom spray. The smell was literally infecting the entire office! There was a slight breeze that day and I quickly made sure I was upwind and out of its way. It was all I could do to stop from throwing up! Think of the worse smell you've ever experienced and triple it. My eyes started to water…and I realized the strong pungent ammonia odor was cat urine; this woman was covered in cat urine! That explained the raincoat, ewww!

She started talking the same way she did on the phone- fast and loud. She walked towards an old, vaguely yellow Volvo in our parking lot and without taking a breath, she waved me to follow. As long as I stayed upwind from her I was ok. She seemed harmless enough except for that odor and it was deadly. The closer we got to the car I noticed something in it was moving slightly and I thought she might have a grandchild in a car seat… poor child I thought, I hope she cracked the window when she arrived. She got to the driver's side door and when she opened it the fumes escaped like hot air coming out of a balloon and I swear it was so potent that you could actually see it flowing out of the vehicle. If the odor on her was like a drop of gasoline on your shoe, then what was coming out of her car was a refinery. It was enough it forced me to stop in my tracks a good ten feet from the car. It wasn't until she stood up after reaching in the front seat for another file folder I saw what was causing the motion in her car- it was CATS! They were jumping from the back seat into the front and sitting on the dash as well as in the back window- there must have been at least a dozen of them! How in the hell did she not smell this? And if she did, how was she not reacting?

She turned to hand me the file she had retrieved and it was already soaked up in the distinct odor from her and the car. To make matters even grosser, I could see stains on the manila folder I'm certain was presents left from at least two of her driving companions. Okay, this woman obviously had some issues. In an effort to not have to take this file, I again told her I wasn't certain that I could not help her. She continued on as if I had said nothing; saying again if she didn't get paid she couldn't take care of her "babies" because they were hungry and she needed to get them food and how the kittens would need some milk. By now I knew that she wasn't ready to hear anything I had to say. I let her ramble on hoping eventually she'd run out of things to tell me.

She told me how she got involved in FUN because she knew Richard and he used to help her with her cats. She even said she had bought into the program and had already received her payoff which she used to help raise and rescue her animals. Richard moved to California and she continued doing the books for FUN, and it wasn't until the last 3 months or so that he stopped sending her a paycheck. She didn't want me to help her expose a fraud- she wanted me to help get her paid. This guy knew who he was targeting for help; he paid her off so she'd believe in the organization and if she did talk who would be crazy enough to believe her?

This was getting weirder and weirder and I just knew she wasn't going to take no for an answer, but it was obvious this case was not for us. My next thought was to throw an inflated fee at her and maybe that would be enough to ward her off. But before I could get this out my mind I went to another thought; maybe she was loaded and no amount was going to scare her, then what? But I had to try.

"Look, I would love to help you out, but honestly like I said before I don't think there is much I can do for you. And it could be really expensive to…" she cut me off mid-sentence.

"How expensive?"

Oh no. Was she filthy rich? How was I going to get her to understand I was not the guy to help her out? Don't get me wrong, it's not I make a habit of blowing off potential clients but Cat Lady wasn't playing with a full deck, one sandwich short of a picnic, a few beers short of a six pack, out to lunch, nutty as a fruit cake, the lights are on but no one's home, she has a screw loose, not the sharpest knife in the drawer, you know, the lift doesn't go to the top floor...

I'm not being mean. This woman needed help beyond what I could give her. The obscene cat odor was a big hint and her traveling companions were another indication of what we'd be dealing with if we took her on as a client. Even if we could help, which we couldn't. I decided now was a good time to ask the question that had been on my mind since she walked in the front door.

"I've got to ask. What's with the hat? Did you make it yourself?"

This hat was different; it wasn't a ball cap, cowboy hat, beret, fedora, knit hat, or a top hat. It was a vegetable strainer. A basic kitchen strainer that was wrapped in tin foil, and oddly enough the more I got to know her the less bizarre it appeared. But her answer convinced me that I was making the right call.

"I can't have the government reading my thoughts!"

"No, no we definitely can't have that." What else could I say?

I felt bad for her. She wanted help and I knew no one was going to give her as much time as I had already. I told her I would look into it but I couldn't make any promises. We took her on with a $150 retainer (which was cash that she actually brought with her). At least that would cover my time. My intent was to make a few phone calls and see if I could help her get her paycheck. Then I would turn the FUN information over to the Feds and let them decide if they wanted to do the work and shut this scam down. Not much else I could do.

The next day I poured myself a fresh cup of coffee and sat down at my desk with the files she gave me in front of me; well, to be honest it was copies of the files. They stunk so unbelievably horribly there was no way they could stay anywhere in the office. I glanced through the papers and found a cell number circled, which just so happened to be Mr. Byrne's. What the heck, might just take a phone call from an outsider to convince him to pay up. Yeah, I know this was hopeful thinking, but I figured we suffered enough at our first meeting so maybe, just maybe, this would be that simple.

I dialed the number and to my surprise a man answered but it was anything but simple. I introduced myself and said I was contacting him on her behalf. I didn't mention I was a PI seeing as I didn't think this would be helpful. I merely suggested he pay his employee for what she had currently earned. He didn't take my suggestion very well. He went off on me and threw around words that I didn't warrant; trust me I know when I deserve them and most of the time I'm doing my best to provoke them but this was not the case at all. I had had enough.

"Look! Maybe you should pay your employee or I just might share these files with the Feds."

That was my intent all along but I wouldn't have tipped him off if he hadn't pissed me off. I hung up on him and made my next call as promised and turned all the files over to the authorities- what would happen next was up to them.

After a bit more research into the FUN organization and a quick consult with a lawyer we trust, it all pointed to it being a scam, con, rip-off, and a fraud. She called me the following week and I gave her the same news I did when we first met and that was the last we heard from her. But that wasn't the last time I heard <u>about</u> her.

The weeks and months went by and eventually, so did the odor in the office. Unfortunately we'll never quite be able to get it out of our minds; odd how you can still smell the memory of an odor. I was flipping through the newspaper one Saturday morning before I headed to tee off and there she was staring back at me. It was her alright; except for the vegetable strainer hat which they must have had her remove before they took the mug shot. She had been arrested for animal cruelty. I just about spit up my coffee.

According to the report the authorities found over 430 cats on her property. She had two trailers that she "shared with her babies". The story continued on stating that a large majority of the animals were either severely ill or already deceased and the living conditions were unbearable. A Hazardous Materials team was called in to sort through the trailers, and in cooperation with the local Humane Society, they saved as many animals as they could. The animals would be available as soon as their health allowed them to be adopted.

The reporter asked her about the cruel treatment and she was adamant in saying she "cared for each of them equally and that no one could have loved them more than she did." She stated she had done nothing wrong and felt "the cats loved the houses so much she let them live there even after they were taken to heaven".

Unbelievable! I knew she had issues but this was absurd. I stayed close to the case which because of the brutality, took very little time to close. She was charged with 10 counts of animal cruelty and 10 counts of permitting an animal to go without care. She was fined $1,000, placed on unsupervised probation for two years, and received a suspended 180 day jail term. It was more than obvious to the courts she did not deliberately intend to harm the animals and was recommended to receive psychiatric help. She was also forbidden from having more than 20 pets in her care.

I sat there quietly for a while and reflected on both what I just read and my interactions with her personally. We've often talked about her lingering trait and joked about her protective hat and I knew then that she had mental issues.

It's a struggle sometimes because we just can't help everyone that walks through our door. We can only do the best with what we're given and hope that the truth will prevail. I think that's all that can be asked of any of us.

The Rule: When someone walks in your office with aluminum head gear OPEN the windows, turn on the fans, and get out the disinfectant quick!!

The GOOD: The Federal Agency did decide the FUN Organization was one that deserved their efforts. Unable to personally seize Richard Byrne (yet), they have been able to shut down his endeavors in numerous states and The Friends United Network has "Desist and Refrain Orders" in California and Alabama. Other states are pending.

The BAD: Richard Byrne continues his efforts and probably won't be stopped until people quit buying into his scams.

The UGLY: The Cat Lady moved out of Idaho and was arrested in 2011 in Montana for similar charges. This time she was housing over 100 cats. Charges are pending.

Rule #9:

STRIVE TO FIND THE TRUTH

"Deadly Motorcycle Accident

The police department says one man is dead after a fatal collision between a motorcycle and a pickup truck.

The accident happened around 5:35 p.m. Friday in the 2300 block of Andaman Way. When police arrived at the scene of the crash witnesses were performing CPR on a 33 year old male. The man was later pronounced dead and police are not releasing his identity until next of kin is notified. The investigation was eventually handed over to the State police.

Police say that a preliminary investigation indicates the victim was Southbound on Andaman Way when a Ford pickup driven by 60 year old David M. Underwood turned out of US Bank parking lot onto Andaman Way heading Northbound. It appears that the driver of the motorcycle attempted to stop by laying down his bike but collided into the driver's side door of the pickup. Underwood was not injured in the accident.

Alcohol or speed does not appear to be factors in the crash. The State police are continuing to investigate the collision."

This story caught my attention as I was sipping my morning coffee my wife brought me before tee off one Saturday morning.(If you haven't noticed I love golf and coffee) I was curious since it happened in front of the store I take my boys when we gear up for our annual fishing trip. What I didn't know was it was going to show up on my desk Monday.

The man was in his sixties and according to his lawyer he was a model citizen. I know, I know most attorneys say that about their clients but I've worked with this particular lawyer enough to know that if he says it, chances are its true. His client was indeed attempting to travel north as the newspaper reported and the cyclist did a T-bone into the side of his pickup; however he does not believe that the involuntary manslaughter charges his client was facing were warranted.

The job of an attorney is to prove to the courts their client is telling the truth. My job is to find the truth-period. Regardless of who's telling it, I make that blatantly clear to every client I meet. If I decide to take their case they are required to sign a contract which clearly states this in section seven:

> *"CLIENT understands that knowingly supplying false, misleading or incomplete statements or information to AGENCY relating to said assignment will result in immediate termination of said assignment and forfeiture of all retainers and money paid to AGENCY. AGENCY does not draw conclusions, make representations, nor expresses any opinions regarding the information contained in the report."*

This not only weeds out those that are hoping I'll help them pull one over on the law but more importantly it states what our intent as a company truly is. The attorneys we work with know this which, in all honesty, is why they hire us in the first place.

The police investigation and report sucked. It was vague and inconclusive based on what little details they had. It occurred on an extremely busy street during Friday rush hour on a spectacular summer day- and they managed to interview a whopping three people. None of them, mind you, actually saw the crash. They either heard the bike then saw the crash on the ground or they saw the bike then heard the crash. Not one of their witnesses actually saw the accident as it happened. There were numerous people there that they could have, and should have, talked to.

I kept reading through the report and looked at the pictures of the accident sight. Then I read the autopsy report and that's when I realized nothing really added up. The cause of death was narrowed down to "trauma to the head". The report detailed the broken bones and internal damage but what it listed next is what struck me as odd. It said the rider had "multiple lacerations on his back". Nothing in the police report had led to this injury. So what's with all the cuts?

He was an experienced rider who not only wore his helmet but also full leathers as well. It didn't add up. How does one get multiple lacerations on his back if he t-boned into the side of the truck? And how was 'speed' not an issue? The motorcycle was the Crotch Rocket Monster 1100. The bike on the wish lists of many a motorcyclist enthusiast. I'm not saying you have to go fast on this bike but I am saying that it's hard not to. There were just too many holes in this report. Nothing irks me more than sloppy police work and there was so much at stake for this lawyer's client. The truth needed to be found, so I agreed to take the case.

The very next day I met with David Underwood. Despite his apparent weary exterior he looked me in the eye and shook my hand firmly. A lot can be told from a handshake and I was impressed by our first encounter. With a confident grasp he introduced himself as Dave and we entered the conference room in my office. He was visibly shaken by the incident but any decent person would be so I wasn't letting that affect my assessment. He sat across from me with slightly drooped shoulders and folded his hands and rested them on the table. I simply asked him to tell me what happened.

He took in a deep breath to help him sit up straighter and even though he probably told this story a hundred times, it still appeared to shake him up.

"I was at my bank going over some paperwork with the manager. I lost my wife three months back and we're working out some financial details."

"I'm sorry to hear that."

"Thank you. That's been hard enough … now this." He took another deep inhale and got back on track.

"Anyway, I was waiting to turn left and head back home. I swear that I thought the lane was clear, so I rolled out. I wouldn't have gone if I didn't. Then I heard the rev of an engine and before I could turn to see what it was I felt him hit the truck door." He exhaled and dropped his head taking a long pause.

"So you were crossing traffic?" I knew the answer but I needed him to keep talking and thought it best I just ask the questions and let him respond.

"Yeah, he was heading south and the bank is on the west side of the road so I had to cut over his lane."

"Was traffic heavy?"

"Yeah it was just after 5:30 and Friday so lots of people were heading home and getting ready for the weekend I suppose."

I paused and waited to see if he would continue on without my prying.

"It was a sunny day and the weekend was supposed to be one of our warmest that summer so I guess lots of folks were getting ready for that."

I didn't want to ask my next question but would be remiss if I didn't.

"Is it possible that you were distracted seeing as you were dealing with some issues from your wife's passing? Maybe you just weren't paying close enough attention? Isn't that possible?"

"I'm not going to tell you that I don't miss my wife because I do, every day. But I swear to you that I thought it was clear. I thought it was clear."

Dave detailed out his memories of that day and answered any questions I had. When I asked if he remembered seeing a particular person or thing that might be relevant, he paused for only a split second before mentioning the woman in the car that would have been immediately in front of him if he had made the full turn north.

"That's great. What was she driving?"

A spark of hope, this could be the break we need. That's what I thought until he gave me the answer.

"A white minivan."

Huh!? So much for a spark. There has to be at least twenty white minivans at any given time on any given road in any given state. There is no other vehicle more common than a white minivan. And to add to the mystery Dave couldn't remember if it had Washington or Idaho plates, or were there any bumper stickers, dents, or anything that would segregate this white van from any other van. We talked for over an hour and even though I was able to get a better picture than I had it still wasn't much to go on. My next move was to head over to the scene of the accident and check things out for myself.

I deliberately made my first (of many) trips to this street in the middle of the morning. I wanted to check out the area without too much traffic and take pictures without distractions. I started at the most northern part of the street and took notes of the businesses as well as pictures. I decided to go down the west side then come back up on the east and end up right where I had begun. I parked in the first business which was a competing bank of Dave's, next to it was a pizza restaurant, then a large mini storage facility with U-Haul rentals. Next to the U-Haul rental was a smaller building occupied by a beauty and tanning salon, followed by a coffee drive-thru hut sharing the same lot. Then there was Dave's bank. I made a mental note to come back to that lot in a bit and take more photos when I was done with the whole tour. Next to his bank just so happened to be Raven's, the fishing store I take my boys to and the last building on the west side was a hardware store. I waited for traffic and the light like a good, law-abiding citizen then crossed and headed up north on the east side of the road. The first business on this side was another restaurant- a little more upscale than the pizza joint, and then a women's clothing boutique that I'm sure my daughter would love. Next was the lighting store, followed by a grocery store, and finally a dentist's office that shared parking lots with a well-known corner drug store.

I took lots of notes and even more pictures before driving over to Dave's bank. I entered into the parking lot and immediately turned around to leave role playing what Dave said he did. As I turned my head to check left for any oncoming traffic I was surprised to see my view was almost completely blocked by a banner for the drive-thru coffee shack promoting "Mocha Monday" and all the other weekly specials. It was attached to a metal post that looked like it was put there specifically for that sign, and the other end was nailed to a rather large power line pole. It blocked enough of my view that I put a call in to the city and made them aware of it. I managed to take plenty of pictures of the banner and even took a short video using my phone of a cyclist pedaling towards me and it was ridiculous how she disappeared while behind the banner.

The skid marks on the pavement were still extremely visible and the traffic was slow enough that I was able to measure them myself. My measurements just so happened to match the police report and I was comforted to know they at least got that right. I measured fifty-six feet and then further at fifty eight feet I noticed a rather large gouge in the road that I didn't notice on the initial police report. It had to have come from the motorcycle, so I took plenty more pictures of it and reminded myself to look for damages when I took a look at the bike. Maybe a handlebar or pedal caused it? Both would leave a sizable gash that could easily match this one. I was already doing the math in my head and realized that there is no mathematical way "speed was not a factor" in this accident. The speed limit on the road was thirty-five miles per hour. For skids to be this long he had to have been traveling faster. At thirty-five mph, even if he was surprised, an experienced driver like he was could have braked or at least swerved around the truck. Dave drove a smaller Ford pickup. It was a red four-door Explorer with a short bed, which would have been easier to maneuver around, let's say, its bigger F-150 or F-250.

My next trip was the very next day, which happened to be a Friday. I made certain to be there at exactly 5:30 pm. I parked in the parking lot of Dave's bank and walked the street observing drivers and vehicles. I knew it was a long shot but just maybe our white minivan worked around here and was taking her usual route home after a long work week. I wasn't ruling out any possibilities. Dave described her and I at least had a little bit of an idea what she looked like. At the time he saw her she was a dirty blond with shoulder length wavy hair and wearing white sunglasses. I only say "at the time" because I'm aware of how quickly hairstyles change on the women in my house and their friends so I knew nothing was for certain here either. For all I knew she could now be a short-haired brunette with black wired-framed glasses. It was almost as long of a shot as finding the white minivan, but I try to never give up hope. Plenty of white mini-vans went by with drivers that didn't necessarily fit the description but I took the plates down anyhow and followed up on those in case someone else just happened to be driving it that day. I got to the end at the corner drug store and started my door to door canvassing.

The bank across the street was the farthest business from the accident and even though employees heard about the crash no one actually witnessed it. That was the theme from the majority of the people I spoke with. The buzz about the accident was surrounding the whole street and I managed to get a few people that heard it- either the motorcycle revving or the crash itself. Almost everyone was cooperative except one and this was at the beauty salon. I walked in and gave my same opening line to the young and large burgundy hair receptionist. I handed her my business card and her demeanor completely changed. She sat up straighter. She folded her arms across her ample chest, and with a snap in her tone told me the owner was not in and wouldn't want to talk to me even if she was.

"Why wouldn't she want to talk to me? She doesn't know who I am or what I want yet."

She maintained her tough, bitchy exterior and informed me that maybe I should try and call her first and not just drop in. Well we all know that wasn't going to happen, especially since she had such an attitude with me. I would certainly be back there and maybe even more than once if need be.

A little stunned by the bizarre response I walked up to the drive-thru coffee hut and got an ice tea before continuing on to the other businesses. I was tempted to go into Raven's Sporting Goods but was able to maintain composure and carry on despite the many "Summer Clearance" posters. The east side of the street started off similar to the west (minus the cold shoulder). People either heard the brakes or came out to see the crash or knew someone who knew something. Nothing was helpful until the lighting store. The manager was standing up front and when I asked if he had seen anything that day he was more than eager to help.

"No, I didn't. I was inside the store when it happened."

Well that's not exactly helpful.

"…but my wife and son saw everything! They were leaving here when it happened."

"Really?! Can you tell me, uh, what does your wife drive?"

"Yea sure, it's an older white minivan."

Hallelujah! He gave me her name, their home phone, as well as her cell phone. I continued on the remainder of the street with no luck other than talking to one witness who claimed he gave his statement to the police. He was the dentist near the end on the east side of the road. Why didn't I read his report? He gave me his full name and number which I could have read by turning around and looking on the front door of his clinic, but I was a little sidetracked by the minivan discovery. I later compared names on the police report and other than matching the first few letters and the last numbers of his business phone, absolutely nothing else matched. How would the police ever have contacted him if need be? They had his information so jacked-up it wasn't even funny, and even worse, he told me that his mom saw the whole thing with him but the cops didn't bother to question her!

"I guess they thought she was too old to remember the details. Hell, she remembers more than I do!"

I left that neighborhood and felt pretty pleased with my efforts. A few businesses had employees there the day of the accident, but were off until Monday morning, so I planned on revisiting them. Plus, I was definitely coming back to figure out why someone I had never met before "didn't want to talk to me".

I went directly home after my door-to-door canvassing and took a few minutes while the grill warmed up to sort through my notes and the pictures as I sat in the shade on the deck enjoying a well-deserved, ice-cold brew. I had a much better visual of the area and accident site but still had a lot of unanswered questions. Like how did he get those back cuts? And why wasn't the mother interviewed? And most importantly, who doesn't want to talk to me? I'm a decent guy; well, unless you have something to hide. I wish I could charge for all the time I spend thinking about a case when I should be relaxing.

The salon opened at ten and I was there at 10:05 hoping to meet the owner, and I did. She was aloof to say the least. She had the same arms-crossed, back-arched posture and must have had a pretty good description of me from her not-so-little helper because I never even got my name out.

"I don't want to talk to you!"

"Fine. Mind if I ask why?"

"You're trying to get that truck driver off and he needs to pay for what he did!"

“You’re right he does.” Her body language immediately quieted as her arms fell to her side and she turned to face me.

“If he was at fault, then you’re right he should pay. But if he isn’t and it truly is just a horrific accident then he doesn’t deserve to.”

That at least opened the door for a conversation and after a few more bouts back and forth I convinced her that I only wanted the truth. Just when I thought she was about to share something she flipped back into her original demeanor and once again “didn’t want to talk to the likes of me”. Something was here, but I’d have to figure that out on another visit. She wanted me out, so I left.

The other employees who supposedly were there the day of the accident had no more words of wisdom to help my case. Matter of fact there was one gentleman and I’m using "gentleman" lightly, who had many words and not an intelligent one among them. He was a small portly man with a Fu Manchu mustache hanging below the corner of his lips and an arrogance way bigger than he was. He was the owner/manager of the storage facility and made certain I understood that he was indeed both the owner and the manager, not an employee as I foolishly referred to him when I first entered his business. He was a pro-biker and I don’t mean a professional. Not only was he pro-motorcycle but what made it worse was that he was anti-car.

He apparently knew the motorcyclist and rode together with the victim. I was compassionate to the fact that he had lost someone he knew, but he came on strong against Dave and already had him tarred and feathered. He rambled on how "that bastard had to pay and how it's old farts like him that makes it dangerous for all cyclists." He was the kind of person that not only thought he knew everything but he needed you to know that he knew everything. I had no time for this idiot and knew that he was not going to be helpful, so I excused myself from his idle rant and left.

My next move was to check out the motorcycle; maybe if I could see the damage I could better explain the gouge in the road and hopefully the injuries to the driver. According to the police report, it was being held at a local bike dealer not too far from the accident so I stopped there on my way back to the office. I wasn't expecting what I found out.

"What do you mean 'you don't have it'?"

The employee who informed me of this immediately went and got his manager, especially after the way I responded. The manager did indeed confirm they no longer were in possession of the bike. When I asked who was, they said they released it to the parents of the driver. I made a call to Dave's lawyer to both inform him of this infraction seeing how evidence in an investigation was not only no longer in the hands of the police, but was also no longer in the hands of the business the police gave it to! He was as unimpressed as I was and after a few phone calls of his own he called me back with what he thought was good news. The bike was not only not at the dealer but it was no longer with the parents either. They had given it to a motorcycle enthusiast friend; and this friend just so happened to own/manage the storage facility on Andaman Way.

"You've got to be kidding me! I just left that idiot."

I hung up the phone and couldn't wait to pay another visit to this owner/manager. He was surprised to see me, and when I came right out and asked to see the bike he lied to my face.

"I don't have it. Who said I have it?"

"Look, I'm giving you a choice. Let me see the bike and I'll leave quietly or, keep playing this game and I'll get the bike put back into evidence and you won't see it again."

"I own it!"

I just love when the cowards cave into pressure.

"I don't care. It's evidence in an investigation and I can get it back where it belongs with one phone call. You decide."

I held up my cell phone and fake dialed for effect; I knew that would get him. He growled under his breath and snatched the keys from the counter. He started walking towards the storage units out back and I followed. He rambled on as he walked steps in front of me about a friend of his nephew who knew someone that saw the whole thing and said he heard that the driver of the truck actually aimed into the motorcycle. He continued on as I silently waited for him to open the metal roll-up door. There it was pieced apart on a canvass throw tarp on the floor of a vacant storage unit. I so wanted to put this idiot on the stand.

"I was fixing it up so you won't be able to find anything."

I again let him rant on without saying a word in return; he watched me snap pictures and when I picked up the foot peg he told me what I suspected.

"That's the left one. The right one was pretty much trashed. I have to buy a new one; I think this one dug into the ground when he laid it down."

That's exactly what I thought happened. So now I had one question answered. I took a few more pictures and left as soon as I felt I had what I needed. The silent treatment I was deliberately giving him was driving him crazy, as I knew it would. He has the type of personality that needs to be in control at all times. When I refused to play his way he was lost. He even changed his tactics altogether and was attempting to be nice and befriend me. I just kept silent knowing that would stick in his head for a very long time.

I was starting to feel like I was making some headway but needed to get in touch with the light store's wife. She answered her cell phone on the second ring and was kind enough to meet me at the restaurant at the end of the street in half an hour. I took the time to look around the street and see if I could find anything I may have missed. Other than the coffee banner being gone, everything appeared the same.

She walked into the restaurant minutes after I did and I recognized her from Dave's description. She was quiet spoken, polite, and very enlightening.

"I saw it all and so did my son who was in the passenger seat. He was traumatized; it was hard on me too, but it's so much harder for a thirteen year old. He shouldn't have to deal with this. We've been talking to a grief counselor and now my son swears he'll never ride a motorcycle. My husband grew up around motorcycles and for me it was a great part of my childhood on the farm. I just don't want this experience to rob him of the same memories. And someone lost their son. It's sad, just all very sad."

I comforted her and we compared notes on teenage boys. I could tell she knew I was sincere and wanted to help me in any way she could. I asked her if she would mind if I recorded our conversation. She didn't mind, and we sat there over coffee for almost an hour as she told me what she witnessed.

"I heard it first really. Traffic was backed way up like it usually does on a Friday, especially in the summer. It's great for our business-good exposure, but I can see how it could get frustrating day in and day out. I usually have the windows rolled up and the air conditioning on but our car is old and if it's idling for a long period of time my husband told me not to run the air. I was okay with the windows open 'cause a nice breeze was blowing."

I sat quietly and listened to her recollect the day. She was adding a lot of other information but I didn't mind, if she needed to do that to keep her thoughts straight, I could be patient. The waitress refilled her cup and she continue on.

"It sounded like he needed to shift, I remember that sound, and that was the first thing I thought when I heard it. I looked over just in time to see his left hand return to the handle bar. The back wheel started to lift off the pavement and my first thought was that he panicked and squeezed the front brake by accident. In a split second I heard the screech of the brakes and watched the front wheel snap to his left then he flew over the top of the bike."

She paused and hung her head as the memory came back to her. I stayed quiet.

"He flew by our window like he was Superman. I think back now and wonder if I could have reached out and grabbed him. I know that sounds silly but it just felt like I could have done that. I swiveled around to follow him but lost him until I looked in my side mirror and saw the bike jammed under the red truck."

"Jammed?"

"Yeah, it slid under the truck but got hung up on something. I wanted to turn around, but there were so many people I knew someone would call the authorities. I just really wanted to get our son home."

She felt the need to defend herself for not sticking around but I reassured her she was not at fault and continued on with some more questions.

"You said you saw his left hand return to his handle bars; where was it?"

"I don't know. I thought maybe he was just waving at someone. It didn't look like he was out of control before that."

We left the restaurant and I thanked her for her time and insight. She offered to help if we needed anything further and I told her we just might considering she was the only one so far that actually witnessed the entire accident. It was about a 40 minute drive back to the office and I played her scenario over in my head.

I needed to take some time and wrap my head around everything, so I asked not to be disturbed and I locked myself in the conference room. I laid out the pictures, reviewed my notes from interviews and re-looked at the autopsy report. It took very little time to put it all together once I had everything in front of me. I knew what happened and I could almost prove it. Almost, but I needed to make one more trip back to Andaman Way.

It hit me when I was laying out the businesses on the street. The wife said she had just left her husband's parking lot which was on the east side of the street. She simply turned right in the north-bound lane and traffic slowed to a halt. Dave's bank was south of this lighting store on the other side of the street, which meant he had to turn left and cross the south bound traffic. There were only two other businesses across from the lighting store that would have had the best view of the cyclist right before he slammed on the brakes; the drive-thru coffee hut and the salon. That's where I headed.

She noticed me immediately and before she could attempt to kick me out I made my point.

"I know you saw the crash and I know you can help us find the truth. That's all I'm trying to do."

She was exhausted and I could tell that the accident was weighing heavy on her.

"Tell me what you know. Help me find the truth. What happened that day?"

That was the push she needed and she immediately broke down in tears. We sat down in the back of the salon and she gave me the missing piece to the puzzle. She was acquainted with the rider; they met at a party a few months back and had kept an ongoing flirtation between them. The fact was he saw her outside and revved up his engine to get her attention. She saw him and waved and that's when he did the same. She turned and walked into the salon only to hear the crash seconds later. She ran to the sight as many spectators did and saw two men giving him CPR. She said she felt so horrible that she left right away and it wasn't until the next morning she heard he didn't make it.

My theory was right and she just proved it.

He was traveling faster than the posted speed limit, got distracted and was not paying attention to the traffic. He slammed on his brakes way too hard and the front wheel jerked to the left and when it hit a right angle, the bike immediately stopped and he was catapulted over the handlebars. He did indeed physically hit the side of the truck. Except when he fell to the ground his bike skidded into him and forced him under the truck. This caused the sever lacerations on his back as well as the gouge in the pavement. Even without the sign blocking Dave's view he was correct in assuming the lane was open and anyone in his position would have pulled out exactly the same way as he did.

I prepared my findings and went to the prosecutor with Dave's lawyer. I presented him with the police findings, which he already was aware of. He then compared them to mine. He was pissed. In his position he counts on law enforcement to do a thorough job so he can best represent the public. This report from the State was useless! The charges of involuntary manslaughter were dropped and he received a failure to yield citation which is the only tarnish he has on his record to date, not even a speeding ticket.

The Rule: Law enforcement officers have a DUTY to get it right, not to come up with a theory. Then only look for information to support it.

A man lost his life and that's a high price to pay. The intent of our investigation was not to desecrate a dead man's name or to prove our client's innocence. It was to find the truth. Responsibility needs to fall on the appropriate party. The driver paid for his mistake with his life, but that does not mean that an innocent man should lose his.

This was an accident- a pure and simple accident. I realize it's human nature to want someone to blame when we lose loved ones, but it should never be an innocent someone and that's what Dave would have been. He had more on the line than a record; he could have lost his job, his home, and everything else in his possession. He didn't deserve this and it was not going to bring anyone back to life.

We find the truth. Sometimes it works in our client's favor and sometimes it doesn't. Regardless, we find the truth.

Rule #10:

DO YOUR JOB – WHATEVER IT IS

When we become adults we get a job. We get our own place, our own car, nice clothes, and nice things to start living on our own. That's when we get bills; and that's why we get a job. We're rewarded for doing our job well with a paycheck. If we do our job poorly then we should either not get a pay check or get fired. It's as simple as that. It doesn't matter if you like your work, you're expected to do it regardless and do it well. This case boils down to that exact philosophy- do your damn job.

Marcel Morgan was a 20-year old Native American, but preferred to be called an Indian. He lived in the county over from ours in a small town where he was born and raised. Well, born anyway. To say he was raised would be a long stretch. He lived an unfortunate life, too rough for most of us to imagine. He basically lived on the streets from his early teens and was in and out of trouble even earlier than that. His mother was that in name only, and he was never sure which of the drifters that came in and out of his house as a kid was his father. He had one he told others was Dad but it's not like they ever took in a ball game or went fishing on the weekends. His grandma was the one who took care of him the most of the time. For him, his friends became his family. He and three others were family for as long as he could remember.

Now the old saying is you can't pick your family but you can pick your friends. That's not saying your friends necessarily will be better than your family. These three grew up in similar situations, even though Marcel won the prize as far as whose family was the most dysfunctional and destructive. They each had jobs, nothing major, just enough to keep beer in the fridge. Two of them lived together in a duplex, the other was a bit younger and still lived at home, and Marcel would often crash in the basement suite of some guy he did odd construction jobs for.

They worked on the weekdays and partied on the weekends usually looking for something to get into, which they could easily find. One particular Friday night the booze was flowing and Marcel and one of his pals found themselves drinking with the same girl on their minds. Well, you inhale enough alcohol and no level of friendship can win over a chick! The two ended up in a fistfight, and before long neither of them got the girl and each was taken home by the other two mutual friends to sleep it off. This was not an unusual event. Maybe it was a little more intense than some of the other altercations but they always kissed-and-made-up and the friendship, as peculiar as it was, remained intact.

Saturday came, and Marcel was on his way over to last night's sparring partner's place when he got a call from him. His friend told him to stop and pick up a bag of rice for dinner.

"Hey man, my debit card won't work. I don't know what's wrong with it."

"I don't care. If you want to eat pick up a bag of rice or don't show." Click.

The three who were already at the duplex knew this was a joke. Its crap they pulled on each other all the time. Not one of them thought twice about it. Well the three at the house didn't, but Marcel did. For some unexplained reason this call set him off. He was already considered the hothead in the group, but this time was different. Something snapped.

Marcel drove home to get cash, and then went to a well-known chain store. He proceeded to buy a bandana, a shot gun, and a box of ammo! Snapping… He made a call to another acquaintance, one who just so happened to hate one of his long time pals, and that's all it took to convince this acquaintance to help him out.

Marcel drove his car, a beat-up teal green 1994 Pontiac Grand Prix he "borrowed" from his granny, and his counterpart followed him in his pickup truck. He led him to a field in the middle of nowhere, parked his Pontiac, grabbed the gun and the box of ammo, and jumped in the front of the pickup.

The driver stared at the shotgun in a way that begged a question, so Marcel answered:

"I got something in town I gotta do and all I need you to do is drive."

The driver was easily convinced seeing as it had something to do with an enemy of his. When asked, after the fact, the driver told cops that he thought Marcel was just going to scare the dude, that's why he agreed to drive him to the duplex.

Sitting in the street, Marcel tied the blue bandana around his nose and mouth bank robber style. After pumping the gun, he exited the truck and walked to the porch. He rang the doorbell and stepped back onto the lawn. The door opened, and the second he knew it was the friend who asked for the rice he fired the gun!! The shot hit the friend in the face and he immediately dropped to the ground. Marcel stepped over him and fires two more rounds in the house - aiming in the direction where he thought the other two were! Luckily, upon hearing the first shot, they instantly threw themselves on the floor; one behind the couch and the other behind the counter in the kitchen. Neither of them was hit. Marcel lowered the barrel and, once again, stepped back over his friend and left in the truck!

The driver wisely said nothing. You know he had to be thinking; "if this guy can shoot his longtime friend he wouldn't hesitate to plug my ass", which is why he decided to remain silent. They drove to Marcel's car where Marcel threw the gun and accessories in. The other driver left his truck parked there and jumped in with Marcel. The two carried on with their Saturday like nothing unusual had happened.

Miraculously, Marcel's victim lives, and is conscious enough in the ambulance to tell them he knows who shot him! Now one thing about Marcel, other than the fact that he was a sizeable man with significant muscle mass, was he had an extremely prominent forehead. His natural hairline was further back than the norm and with his black hair short and buzzed like he kept it, his forehead was even more apparent; nothing a bandana could ever disguise.

"It was Marcel Morgan. He drives a green Pontiac but was in a blue Toyota tonight with someone. I couldn't see the driver's face."

The EMTs continue to do their job and anticipated him going into shock soon even though he shared this information in a bizarrely calm fashion with the officer on scene. In turn, the officer got on the radio and shared this with all of the local police. I got a chance later to look at the x-rays of the face and it was interesting, in a very morbid way. The shots hit him on the right side of his face and exploded from the bridge of his nose to over to his ear. The film detailed what looked like fifty to sixty small spherical pellets impacted into his face. Amazing, really, that he lived, let alone held a conversation on the way to the hospital! Lucky for our victim that #7 shot out of a twelve-gauge shotgun is not a very effective weapon for killing people; works good on birds though.

A BOLO went out through the county as well as the adjoining ones assuming Marcel was on the run, but he wasn't! Not only was he not on the run, but he and his driver were heading for a beer at the same place where the fight was the night before! Minutes after hearing the BOLO over the radio, a cop spotted Marcel's car on the main drag and the lights went on. The local police knew his car even without the description; they'd been involved plenty of times before with minor violations. He was well known and not well liked by the authorities.

There was no cause to pull him over, he wasn't speeding or swerving, but with the BOLO activated this was all the officer needed. This is where the whole situation went haywire and all the grief which follows starts.

The cop tells Marcel and his buddy to get out of the car, and that they are being arrested in connection with attempted murder. Marcel comes unglued and from the minute the cop spins him around against the hood of the car he doesn't shut up. He's screaming profanities and spewing threats to have his badge! A second cop arrives and that doesn't stop his ranting. Unfortunately, with all his mouthing off the officer fails to finish reading him his Miranda Rights; he can't get a word in edgewise so stops trying.

A quick little history lesson on the Miranda Rights. Everyone knows how it starts, "You have the right to remain silent…" and so on, but not everyone knows what started it. It was created in 1966 as a result of the US Supreme court case of Ernesto Miranda vs. Arizona. In this case the defendant, Miranda, was convicted on kidnapping, rape, and armed robbery charges based on his confession under police interrogation. But because he was questioned in police custody in a room completely cut off from the outside world and was never given a full warning of his rights, his attorney fought the conviction. This battle went on for almost one year; long enough that it caused the courts to come up with something to stop this argument from happening in the future. So was born "The Miranda Rights." The good news was that the State of Arizona re-tried him and he was convicted.

It's because of this case there is a requirement that a suspect must be informed of their legal rights at the time of arrest. Without this warning suspects have a potential loophole, and unfortunately that's what this cop gave Marcel. And to make matters worse, Marcel knew it.

When I was a cop in the military I carried these rights on a card and had it laminated. I kept it tucked in my wallet and whenever I needed to "Mirandize" someone I pulled it out and read it word for word. I didn't do this because I couldn't remember the words; I did it so there would never be a doubt that I did my job! When I was called to testify and asked if I read the defendant their rights I told them that I pulled this card out of my wallet (and I'd show it to them) and read the words verbatim.

Regrettably that wasn't enough damage for our "cowboys." They then proceeded to tell Marcel they were going to search his car.

"Bullshit! You have no reason to search squat. I didn't do anything!"

Well, not only was he right but the cop did the search anyway. And yes, he happened to find the gun and the ammo and even the blue bandana. But because he didn't have enough probable cause or a search warrant, none of it was admissible in court! Matter of fact it's like it didn't even exist. Bottom line…the cop failed to do his job correctly and we all potentially could pay for it.

It begs the question, why? Inexperience or ignorance? What they legally should have done *first* was read him his rights (duh), second they should have impounded the car and sealed it with evidence tape. Next, all they would have had to do was call a tow truck. After getting the statement from the victim they could go to the judge and prove probable cause to search the vehicle and he would grant them a search warrant. Done deal; then everything found was found legally and is usable in court.

If they would have done their job… it would have ended that night. But it didn't and that's when we entered the case. The court appointed Confidential Investigations to investigate on the defendant's behalf. By the time we were called, Marcel and his accomplice had been in jail almost six months.

Marcel was being held on three counts of first-degree attempted murder and the driver was charged with one felony count of first-degree rendering criminal assistance.

Beth and I worked the case and met with Marcel's attorney the next day. Beth was an investigator who worked a for us before retiring (for the second time). She was a detective with a local law enforcement agency and was instrumental in knocking down drug crimes in our areas. We were grateful to have her join our team after retiring. Her experience and professionalism is something we were blessed to have; and she used both of these qualities while investigating this case. The attorney gave us the detailed police reports, which were abominations. Other than what we've told you above, we discovered no photos were taken of the vehicle and to make things worse, which I never thought could be possible, the two reports written by the on-scene officers who did the "search" contradicted one another! One said the bandana was blue, which it was, while the other said it was red, which it wasn't. They had different times of the day and opposing street names, and items in different locations in the car. *What the hell?* It was as if these two cops were at two totally different arrests.

Once again it begs the question, why? If not inexperience or ignorance, maybe it's a lack of training, or a power trip? Young cops anxious to nail down their first felony arrests? Whatever the reason, there's absolutely no excuse for this level of incompetence. The defense attorney would eat these cops alive, which gives even more power to Marcel and his buddy who had been held for six months, mind you, under these illicit circumstances. I hate to see cases like this but my job is to get to the truth. This gives his attorney the best possible chance of making decisions in the best interest of his client's case.

We listened to all the interviews between Marcel and the police and I had a pretty good idea of what to expect. Every conversation anyone had with him turned into a screaming match. He was smart and knew how to push buttons; he was in control of all the discussions thus far. We listened to at least four different exchanges and he changed his story each and every time. The first time Marcel was interrogated he confessed:

"Hell yah I did it; he had it coming."

He knew damn well they couldn't use any of it since his rights hadn't been read to him. The very next time he changed it up:

"Hell no; I didn't do it. Why would I? He's my friend."

Each story after that got more and more convoluted. The latest and most elaborate version was that he didn't do it but knew who did!

"I told him it was coming but he never listened. He took drugs that he couldn't pay for so they retaliated. Check them out; they're a well-known gang in town. That's who did it, I guarantee it."

His stories flip-flopped so many times they sent him off for a psych evaluation to determine if he was even competent to stand trial. He wasn't crazy- he was playing them. They did the entire workup and he was found capable. He was playing them and winning. The one common denominator of each interrogation was his level of anger; he'd scream and yell and the cops would yell back. Like I said, he was in control.

Beth and I showed up at the jail and did all the official check-in procedures, which included a deputy asking us if we had any weapons. We waited in the attorney meeting room for Marcel to enter. The room was empty except for a small steel table and three equally cold and heavy chairs. The walls were solid concrete painted a muted gray. The table was set up on one side of the room against the wall. The deputy brought Marcel in and sat him in the lone chair directly across from mine; Beth's chair was on the other end but about three feet away. He sat down quietly.

I introduced myself and Beth. I went on to explain we were there to help him and that we worked for his attorney. Anything he told us was protected by attorney client privilege.

"I'm here to find out the truth."

He immediately stood up, forcing his chair to fall back and pounded both fists onto the steel table rattling all four legs.

"I'll tell you the f-ing truth!"

I didn't realize until later on in the conversation Beth had been slowly sneaking her chair closer to me. Based on his escalating actions it wasn't farfetched he was going to come over the table at me and she wanted to be ready! She is a tough lady and anyone would have responded the same way. Not flinching, I sat there unaffected by his rant and I could see this affected him.

"So tell me."

He continued on in an over-the-top loud voice that I'm certain the entire jail facility heard. Still I didn't respond. He decided to stick with the drug dealer story and I let him ramble on acting interested. His tale went on for about fifteen or twenty minutes and his volume kept going up. His arms were waving continually and he wandered off on a couple of tangents about conspiracies against his dad and how the cops are out to get his family. I jotted down some random words on the notepad I had in front of me for effect. It was working; I could tell he was starting to believe we were on the same side of the legal fence. I waited until he took a breath and interjected.

"Here's the good thing about your case. Miranda Rights were not completed."

"I know. I know. Dumb asses."

He said this with a smile that made my skin tingle, but I went on anyway.

"And the search they did…that was just jacked-up." I said.

"I know! They screwed up royally!"

That was just enough fuel to light his fire and off he went again. Only this time he was yelling-throwing profanities and his finger in the air professing his innocence. I remained calm and hadn't even shifted in my chair once during this whole conversation. The only thing I was thinking was I might as well tell his attorney "you win", even though I knew his win was a loss for society. By now Beth was sitting right next to me. But I had to know for certain, so I took him down a different road.

"You know that they didn't do the forensics on your gun. You didn't do it, right? So let's get the forensics done and prove it once and for all. What do you say?" I asked.

They didn't bother to do the forensics because of their first screw up; it wouldn't be admissible in court anyway so why bother....

"You can't do forensics on a shotgun." Marcel stated.

Not the response I was expecting; not the truth either so I set him straight.

"Uh...yes you can."

"No way F#!ker, I saw it on CSI. They can't trace the shots back to a shotgun."

CSI? *Is he serious*? Did he really get his arsenal advice from a Hollywood cop show?

"Look I've been doing this over 20 years and it can and has been done." I cut him off before he could continue on with his television knowledge. "You're right in they can't use the individual pellets but they can use the shell and match it to the firing pin in the gun."

"That's B.S. They can only get that stuff from a rifle." Marcel said.

He was one-hundred percent wrong and I was just the guy to tell him. With a rifle or a pistol the bullet can be traced back to the gun because the rifling leaves tracks or grooves on the bullet that can be easily matched. With a shot gun the barrel is smooth and no tracks are left, but the firing pin that strikes the primer in the shell (which holds the pellets or shots) *does* leave a unique indent that, most definitely, can be traced back to the gun it was shot from. And, when the gun fires, the brass shell gets imprinted with the milling marks on the bolt of the gun. So I reiterated my stand one more time.

"Dude we can so prove that it wasn't your gun. You're innocent right? My job is to work in your best interest. You just give me the go ahead and I can have your attorney compel them to do the forensics and prove it once and for all. So what do you say?"

The silence that followed was even more disconcerting than his rants; it was like watching a bomb. I had just lit the fuse and there was nothing left to do but watch it burn down and take cover. I mentally held my ground and got ready to stay the course; no flinching allowed.

Seconds later, he again flew out of his chair kicking it behind him; I didn’t react. He was now shrieking and we had yet to see his rage level off! He was yelling my direction but not necessarily at me.

“F this! I’m going to kill the judge. I’m going to kill the prosecutor. I’m going to cut the heads off of both my attorneys and leave them to rot on the f-ing court steps. When I get out of here I’m going to kill them all.” Snapping…

Naturally, I’m cleaning it up a bit so throw in as many F-bombs of your own and it still wouldn't be close to what came out of his mouth. But I remained calm and acted as if he had said nothing of importance. The entire jail heard him; there was no way they couldn’t have. I simply raise my head slightly until I caught his attention and asked one more time.

“This is simple. Do I do the forensics or not?”

He voluntarily sat down, took a deep breath and exhaled slowly; a locked stare right back at me. In almost a whisper, he replies.

“No.”

Without saying another word to Marcel, I turned to look directly at Beth, "Ready to go?" And without anything else being said, the deputy escorted Marcel out. We waited until he was gone and then we were also escorted down the same hallway, only Marcel went right to his cell and we went to the lobby. We opened the door to see what had to have been the entire staff, standing there with completely silent, shocked looks on their faces. Again, I said nothing, and let them watch us as we exited the building. Beth remained by my side and it wasn't until we got to the car that she made a sound.

"That was intense! Wholly crap, how the hell did you stay that calm the entire time? That was great. Well, other than the fact that we can't use any of that against him."

She was right. We were hired on his behalf and were under attorney client privileges. I couldn't tell the judge or the prosecutor, even though the entire jail heard his threats. So I'm sure they'd hear about it but not from me. I did, indeed, call his attorney and filled him in on all the happenings. We both agreed that we knew he did the crime, but we also both knew we had our jobs to do and that's exactly what we were going to do. The drive home was quiet.

Beth and I spent the next few weeks chasing shadows but we dug into every possible area of the drug hit story and came up with a big zero.

As we made reports to the attorney on every aspect of the case, it came down to: if Marcel just sits there and keeps his mouth shut you win! Simple as that, and it wasn't because he didn't do it. It was because the cops failed to follow cop 101 procedures.

Today was his pre-trial hearing. Beth came into the office as early as I did. Both of us didn't get much sleep. I offered to buy her breakfast, but we agreed that neither of us were really hungry.

"I can't just sit around and wait."

"It just makes me sick to my stomach. We all know he did it and we know he's going to walk."

"I know." I agreed again. "Just wonder how long it'll take before he kills someone for real."

I convinced Beth that we couldn't fix this, it wasn't our fault. She knew this was true but it didn't help settle the pit in our stomachs. The only thing left to do was wait until he came through with one of his promises, and hope the cops did a better job than last time. He'd be back in jail again, that was a reality, just who would have to pay?

The prosecutor and defense were seated and the Deputies escorted Marcel to the seat next to his attorney. The judge entered the court room and all rose. The official business commenced and they sat down. All he had to do was sit still and shut up.

Before the judge could begin Marcel stood up and started the angry chatter! His lawyer quickly grabbed at his left sleeve in an attempt to silence him, but that only made matters worse!

“I want to fire my lawyers! Both of them! I’ll defend myself!” Marcel was snapping again…

What? Is this really happening? All he had to do was sit and shut up. He had the attention of the entire court room and the judge finally got him to stop talking. The judge called the prosecutor and defense to the bench and even though those in the court room couldn’t hear what they were saying, it had to be about his sanity. Was he capable of defending himself? The prosecutor gladly volunteered the psych evaluation details and I’m certain the Defense did it’s best to object. The Judge over-ruled and found him competent. His main attorney had been fired so the judge ordered the second attorney to stay and assist. His main attorney stood up, gathered his documents, and walked out of the court room. Everyone could literally read the "Halleluiahs" written all over his face. There was a light at the end of this tunnel.

The trial started within days. The Judge turned to 'Mr. Morgan' after the prosecutor had finished and allowed him to make his opening statement. He started with an accusation against the drug dealer. The Judge let him finish then turned to the opposing bench and the prosecution started their case.

Long story short, Marcel was convicted in all three counts of first-degree attempted murder and was sentenced to the maximum punishment of twenty five years, each conviction consecutive. That's 75 years without parole.

All he had to do was sit and shut up; thank goodness he was too arrogant and stupid to do so. He hung himself!

"See, the justice system does work! I also have a bridge for sale, you interested?"

The Rule: If you're a cop you are paid to do a job, so do it. And do it to the best of your abilities. If you can't handle what you've been hired to do then get a job flipping burgers! Blind luck or dumb luck is not good enough when lives are at risk!

Rule #11:

RESPECT THOSE WHO HAVE EARNED IT

We owe a lot to our military men and women. Sometimes we only remember this on a scheduled holiday like Veteran's Day. More times than we should, we fail to recognize struggles they may have to endure when they return to civilization. Not all soldiers struggle, but some do, and it's real.

Our next case involved one such soldier. I received a call from a familiar attorney. He had a client who found himself in an altercation and wanted us to help. This particular attorney is both a good lawyer and a great man. He's been in the business for a long time and has worked hard to earn a reputation of honor and integrity. He also works as a contract conflict public defender. This basically means if the elected public defender has a conflict he cannot ethically take the case; maybe he knows the victim or is somehow related to the accused. This is when a contract public defender is called in. Now, if you're the accused and are assigned a contract defender then you really are getting an amazing deal! Public defenders are usually younger and less experienced attorneys and are over-loaded with cases. You get the benefit of representation from a seasoned, experienced attorney.

This attorney told me his client had been deployed to Iraq, was wounded, and then given an honorable discharge. He had returned home less than 3 weeks ago and hadn't been able to establish steady work, so he couldn't afford very much. I'm an ex-military man myself so I wanted to help this soldier out.

The next afternoon we met in my office. My first impression of the soldier was perplexing. He was tall in stature, well over 6 feet, and stood with a posture in keeping with the military ways. He was strong physically, but didn't carry an over-abundance of muscular bulk. He was polite but shy. He shook my hand with authority but struggled to look me in the eyes. We sat down and I started the conversation.

"So Albert, tell me what happened that night."

He took in a deep breath and forced himself to sit up straight. He advised me to call him Al and then began from the beginning.

"Looking back now I know it was stupid, but it wasn't like they said."

"That's okay, just tell me what happened and we'll go from there."

"Okay. I got back a couple weeks ago and have been having trouble getting back into the swing of things. I don't know why, it just seems harder than I remember. I spent the week looking for work. I started out doing alright but as the week continued I got more and more frustrated. People seem different to me. I know they're not, but to me it just was harder to relate."

I watched as he shifted in the chair, like it was upholstered in tacks, and when he wasn't shifting in the chair his foot was twitching or his fingers were tapping. I've done thousands of interviews and interrogations and am quite proficient in body language. Under any other circumstance I may be forming a conclusion that perhaps he had some guilt; but knowing what I do about the military I came to another conclusion. This soldier has PTSD, post-traumatic stress disorder. His posture and demeanor were a dead giveaway. So I gave him the time to tell his account and didn't put any pressure or time constraints on our conversation.

"Anyway, I decided to blow off a little steam and get drunk. I realize that sounds immature but I want to lay it all out on the line. My intent was to get wasted, so I hired a cab to come get me and my plan was to call the same cab and have it take me home at closing time. I wasn't sure where I was going so I took the cabbie's advice and ended up at a bikini bar."

He paused again almost as if he expected me to cast judgment but when I didn't react, he continued on.

"I was there not even a half hour when this guy came up to me and tried to pick a fight."

"He asked you to fight?" I had heard some of the night's account from his attorney but I was baiting him with questions like this one just to assure his stories were the same.

"Yes sir. I took a seat at the bar and ordered a beer and a shot of Jack Daniels. I finished the shot right away and was working on the beer. He came up on my left and leaned his shoulder into me. I thought it was an accident so I didn't respond, then he did it again and he asked me what I thought I was doing there. I told him I just came for a few drinks and didn't want any trouble. Apparently, I was the new bull in his herd and he didn't like that."

I interjected his thought and asked if he, by chance, provoked him somehow, unintentionally. Maybe he looked at his girlfriend wrong or the guy was anti-military. He assured me that he wasn't there long enough to eye anyone, and that he deliberately doesn't wear anything in public that connects him with the military.

"I never know how people react, some respect the army and some don't, so I dress completely in civilian clothes."

I asked why he went to the bar alone and, again, he had a logical answer.

"I haven't been back long enough to connect with people and I just wanted to be alone and have a few drinks. I wouldn't have been the best company anyway."

"So did you fight?"

"No. The bartender knew this guy pretty well and told him to back off or he'd kick him and his buddies out again. So I assumed he's targeted other guys before. He went back to his friends in the corner and I stayed where I was for the rest of the night."

"You never spoke to each other again?"

"Not until the bar closed; that's when it all happened. It was last call so I called the cab that brought me; the bartender asked me to wait outside so he could close up, so I did. I sat down and waited on the curb. I don't think I was waiting too long, and when I looked down the street for the cab I saw a group of people walking up towards me. I stood up and didn't recognize who it was until he was only a few feet in front of me."

Bullies never travel alone do they? They need to have an entourage to show off to; they need to prove that they're bigger and "bad" to everyone else. Al knew exactly what kind of person he was up against.

"He came right up to me and pushed my chest with both hands. I took a step back and again told him I didn't want to fight. He told me that didn't matter because he did. Then he grabbed my jacket and it turned into a tug-of-war. He tried to throw me down a few times and it was getting pretty rough. His friends were screaming at him to "kick my ass" and that's when I realized there was no getting out of this without fighting back. So I did, sort of."

My original thought when I listened to him detail the night was that the battle came to blows and now the instigator was crying because he lost. Al was a fair-sized man and had military hand-to-hand combat training, so I was anticipating the punch line was going to be that Al was being charged for actually using his training. His opponent wasn't small either. According to Al, he was five or so inches shorter but much wider and definitely worked out.

"So how'd the fight turn out?"

“Well, it didn’t really get to be an actual fight.”

I paused then, same as he did, and waited for him to explain what that meant.

“I didn’t want to scrap. I just wanted to go home but he just kept going on. He was shaking me back and forth so I finally had enough. And I couldn’t break free of him."

I sat there stunned as he detailed out his actions. I could not believe my ears! I’ve been around many scraps and scuffles, and I can honestly say none have had anything as gross as this happen. According to Al, and pictures I saw later confirmed his statement, he reached both his arms up and locked his fingers behind his aggressor’s neck. Then, he forcefully pulled this guy’s face towards his own and with one bite he bit of the guy’s nose off! Not just the tip either, slightly under one inch was missing from the front of his face.

“He dropped to the ground and there was blood everywhere. His friends just stood there staring and I’ll admit I couldn’t believe what I did either. His hands were covering his face and the blood was seeping through his fingers. I panicked and I ran. I got about two blocks away when I realized that I still had his nose in my mouth. I spit it out and ran at least two more blocks. I remember sitting on a curb again and calling the cabbie. I told him that I wasn't at the bar anymore; he never picked me up."

The cab didn't, but the cops did. The police report read like a zombie movie detailing the dried blood on Al's face and jacket; and Al's mug shot was no prettier. He was arrested under assault and battery charges, as well as mayhem, which is the criminal offense for intentionally maiming another person. We use it in everyday terms to describe chaos and disruption. This is kind of the same, only throw in serious malicious injury which makes it a felony offense.

I believed Al and wanted to help even though things didn't look good for him. I had already decided to take his case but wanted to make sure he was as devoted as I was so I cut him a deal.

"I'll work this myself and you're going to help. Anything I need, anytime, you have to be there. I'm also going to drop my fee to $1,000 and, most importantly, you have to get help from the VA."

"Help with what? I don't need help."

His answer was defensive and we both knew what he needed; but I wasn't willing to invest in him if he wasn't willing to invest in himself. So I called his bluff.

"Okay. Have a nice day." I simply stated.

I stood up and opened my office door for him to leave, but he didn't budge.

"That's the deal. Period. This is not negotiable." Again, simply stated.

"Okay." And with that he jumped up and walked out of my office.

Huh? What just happened? I wasn't sure if that meant we did or didn't have an agreement! Less than a minute later the main door opened and now there were two men standing in the lobby. Al introduced his father to me and we all returned to my office. I explained the deal to his dad, who, unbeknownst to me had been waiting in his car this whole time. He was also an ex-military man and also knew his son was struggling. He only wanted what was best for his son and it was obvious by his response.

"I'm in." He wrote us a check and we started our investigation.

I asked if Al happened to have the jacket he was wearing that night. He left with his father and returned with the jacket within the hour. It still had the bloodstain, which is why he said he hadn't worn it since. I turned the jacket over and saw the seams where the sleeves met the body of the coat were either ripped or stretched almost to the point of ripping. This was evidence that we immediately shared with his attorney.

The next day I went down to the bikini bar and started asking questions. Naturally no one saw anything. Bars are notorious for keeping a tight lid on their employees. The owners don't want to have to take responsibility for any personal damages, especially when it's caused by a patron they should have cut off hours ago! So they use the security of the employee's jobs to shut them up; "talk and you walk". I still went through the motions and chatted up as many as I could before I was *not so kindly* asked to leave.

I came away empty-handed, other than the name of the attacker and a few of his followers; that was enough to do some additional research on the computer. What I found didn't surprise me; disturbing the peace, disorderly conduct, domestic violence, DUI, and it ended with the ever-so-disgusting urinating in public. He's a prize alright. His followers were much cleaner, but it was only a matter of time they'd get dirty if they kept hanging with the likes of this delinquent.

I managed to get contact numbers for three of his friends. This wasn't hard really, considering how open everyone is on the social networks. Lucky for us, the stupider people are the more they share. I interviewed them and they each gave me another contact and I interviewed them also. So out of a half dozen witnesses they all saw the same thing. Not just the same thing but the identical same thing. Logic says if the stories are the same then it must be the truth. Well, that's true to a point; matching the general gist of an event is one thing but matching it word-for-word is another. These accounts were in the same order using the same catchphrases; each of them were rehearsed and calculated. I've been doing this long enough to know the difference and this didn't sit well. Reality was, however, this guy had a ton of witnesses on his side and Al had no one. Or so I thought.

A couple of days went by with nothing breaking on this case and then my phone rang. The screen on my phone read "blocked call" and I answered it to hear a young woman on the other line.

"I think I can help you with that army dude." She said.

"Ok, you have my attention."

She started by saying that she didn't want to give her name because, even though she hated the place and the owner more, she needed the job and knew she'd be fired if anyone found out. She was one of the waitresses and was on duty the night of the fight. She confirmed what Al told me about how it started; she was actually behind the bar when this guy came up and tried to start a fight with Al. She said he did his best to blow him off politely and that she and the bartender even joked about how patient he was. She said they laughed and wished that someone would haul off and deck the dude already. Then she continued with the events of the evening.

"I walked him out at closing time and sat him on the curb." (Him, being Al of course…)

"That's funny; Al didn't mention that anyone was with him."

"That doesn't surprise me, he was pretty wasted. I felt bad for him; he seemed like a nice guy yet he sat there by himself all night without a word to anyone. He must have had something fairly heavy on his mind. I just wanted to make sure he got in the cab okay."

"So then you left him there?"

"No. Not yet. I saw the group walking towards us and that's when I ran. I feel terrible and I know that I should have called the cops or something, but I was so scared that I … I just left."

I assured her that I understood why she did what she did. She was right in assuming that, more than likely, they would have targeted her too just because she was sitting with him. She told me about other instances where this same instigator caused trouble for the bar, picking fights with other guys and harassing the girls. It was a hole of a bar and their main source of income comes from deadbeats like this guy, so it's not surprising he never gets anything short of a verbal slap on the wrist. Then she said something I could use.

"I sat in the car and watched the whole thing. I saw another guy from the bar that night watching in his parked car that wasn't too far from mine."

The second watcher was also a regular, but according to my witness he was a nice regular. Not sure that info held a lot of water, but at least we added another member to our team. She hung up, and I immediately retrieved her number so I could call back if I had further questions. I just didn't tell her I had her number. She was freaked out enough, so I didn't want to add to her anxiety by letting her in on the fact I knew how to unblock her call.

The next day I showed up back at the bar, at the time she suggested, and was indeed able to chat with the other watcher. He not only collaborated Al's and the waitress's accounts, but had yet *another* name of someone else who witnessed the incident. It was unanimous; Al was acting in self-defense.

Was biting off someone's nose the best protection? Probably not, but you take enough liquid courage, mix it with equal parts fear and anything can happen. Adrenaline is a mystery rush and we can't always control how we react to it. It's our "fight or flight" response and has been known to motivate mothers to lift cars off their babies! So, biting off another person's appendage may not be that far-fetched. I'm sure, looking back now, Al will think twice before making that same move again. I would also bet he still has that nasty taste in his mouth, and in his head for that matter. With the coat and three witnesses we had enough to build a solid argument to take to the prosecutor.

The Prosecutor conceded and agreed with our findings; the felony charge of mayhem was dropped and he pled to a lesser charge of battery.

The Rule: Act respectable even if you're not! If you don't, then eventually someone is going to teach you a tough lesson!

We live in a world that has a large part of our population willingly grasping for a disorder or syndrome. Almost like being labeled with something excuses us from having to act and behave responsibly. It's an unfortunate fact that some have used and abused this. Parents say their kids have ADHD so they're excused from actually having to do the hard work of real parenting. Adults make claims of depression and medicate instead of taking control of their own destiny.

Therefore, we have to be diligent enough to recognize the frauds and be mindful and empathetic to those who really are suffering. These disorders are real and they need serious medical attention; the same as a cancer patient would. Our military veterans dedicate their lives to our freedom and we should never forget this! Our men and women on the front lines witness traumatic events most of us could never imagine! They do this every day of every month and sometimes for years. So, when you see a soldier in uniform or a veteran shake their hand and thank them for their sacrifices. Unfortunately, some are still paying for those sacrifices.

Rule #12:

BEFORE YOU BUY SOMETHING, MAKE SURE IT'S NOT STOLEN

If you love the outdoors, Idaho is the place to be! Whether you're a biker, hiker, fisher, skier, camper, boater, or rock climber, this state has everything to offer. This is even more accurate if you're a hunter. Whether you're an archery fanatic or a devout gunman, there's always an open season and usually an abundance of game. Well, depending on the harshness of our winter and the population of wolves; but that's a controversy for another time.

Our client was born in Idaho and spent most of his childhood there. He went to college in the South and landed a job in Tennessee right after graduation. He had grown with the same company, and 25+ years later he earned the title of CEO. It's true that once you're an Idahoan you're always an Idahoan. It's tough to leave it behind and when he was at a place in his life where he could afford to get back a little piece of Idaho, he did. With both money and time on his side he found a place where he could come and hunt. He and his late father had spent two weeks of every autumn hiking and hunting in the northern hills of Idaho and that's the exact land he now owned for himself.

It had been almost four years since he had made his hunting dream come true; he was able to purchase a gorgeous 80-acre parcel in the hills he had hiked as a kid. It was a breathtaking piece of property with everything an outdoorsman dreams of: meadows and mountains, as well as a natural stream which ran into a watering hole. For the first two years he had rented a travel trailer and set it up at the bottom of the property. From there, he hiked into the valley where he had strategically placed his tree stand overlooking the watering hole. It was in the second year of sitting on this stand he discovered the perfect place to put a permanent hunting cabin. The solitude and isolation hunters experience while waiting for an opportunity is truly spiritual, especially in a tree stand. Sitting high above what feels like the rest of the world, with nothing but nature and your thoughts, is something that only a fellow hunter can appreciate. Many critical and imperative decisions have been made in this exact environment. We usually find answers in our own silence and solitude which is a part of why hunting is so appealing to some of us. It's more about the silent pursuit in nature than it is the kill.

That season of the epiphany, our client hired a local contractor to make his dream hunting cabin a reality. A concrete slab was poured and electricity and plumbing were brought into the site. After numerous emails and phone calls a perfect hunting cabin was placed on the peak of his property. It was an ideal log cabin, 12' x 26', appropriately called "The Outdoorsman." It was made out of 2" x 6" untreated lodge pole pine with a corrugated metal roof; an amazing mountain getaway! The interior was just as perfect; the front aluminum glass door led to a cozy living room that had an old style pot belly wood burning stove in the far corner. On the left side were steps going up and on the right was a narrow hallway. The hallway led first to a pocket door that enclosed the bathroom, then to a mini kitchen fully equipped with a small sink, stove, fridge, and microwave. The steps went to the sleeping loft which simply had a bed and a small built-in closet. The interior was, of course, done in rustic outdoor colors like green and burgundy with a few bear accents scattered throughout. A small dark brown couch, matching chair, and coffee table sat in the center of the living space. Other than a bed, there was no furniture upstairs. As small as it was square foot wise, it truly seemed bigger inside because of the multiple windows. There was one in the loft, one on the front and back, as well as two on each of the sides. A small deck was added to the front under the 6-foot overhang of the roof. It was perfect simplicity and for a hunter it was, beyond a doubt, ideal.

The next year's hunting season was the best yet and the cabin made it even harder for him to leave when his 2-week hiatus ended. He spent each night on his porch sitting around a fire contemplating everything and nothing. Some would look at a vacation alone in the woods in fear, but for him it was the respite that ignited him for the rest of his year.

Fast forward almost 365 days to September and into elk archery season. Our client flew into the closest airport and rented a four-wheel drive truck, which is the only way he could get to his cabin. If there was already a ton of snow on the ground he had to come up with a backup plan to get him and his gear "home". Fortunately, he'd always managed to beat the heavy stuff which usually falls late October or early November. There was sometimes a dusting when he came but nothing a truck couldn't plow through. He was like a kid on his birthday and couldn't wait to chop wood and start his fireplace! Last year was his first season in his cabin and he had anticipated this return each and every day since!

He landed in the early morning, like he usually did, and wanted to get up there in the daylight with plenty of time to unpack and prepare for the weeks ahead. Later that day, according to the clock, he should have been sitting around his stoked fire enjoying a swill of his favorite bourbon.

Unfortunately, he was not. He was calling our office instead.

"I'm looking for a PI who knows the area."

"I'm very familiar; what can we do for you?"

He started by explaining he was from Tennessee and came up each year for hunting season. He gave me the details of his property and cabin, and I was easily convinced how invaluable this trip was to him. Then he jumped into the sheriff's department and even though he thought they were extremely competent, he said that they only had one detective. That was his problem- his case would unfortunately take a back seat to all the other cases the detective had.

"So what can I help you with?" I asked one more time since I still wasn't certain why he even needed a Private Eye.

"I got off the plane, rented a truck, stopped at the grocery to stock up on food, and headed up to the cabin."

Okay. Still not sure where I fit in so I kept silent hoping he would get to the punch line.

"I got to the gate, unlocked it and drove up the path. Then I turned the corner where you can see the cabin from; well, where you should have seen the cabin."

"Should have?"

"Yup. It's gone."

"What?" I thought he said gone but that's not possible, is it?

"I turned the corner and didn't see it, then when I got closer all there was left was the concrete pad. The rest is gone. Someone stole my cabin and I want you to help me find who."

Well this was a first! A stolen house, that's interesting. Naturally, I was intrigued so I invited him into the office where we could talk further. When he arrived at the office I was pleased to see that I mentally had him pegged pretty close to how he was in person. I guessed late fifties, which he was, he was shorter than I was by about three inches and had a fair size mid-section. He had a grayish beard which looked a little out of place on him so I assumed it only came out during hunting season. He showed me pictures and I immediately got the allure- it was a great getaway. Then he cut to the chase and simply asked:

"Can you do it?"

"It's not a matter of 'if', we definitely can. It's just how much do you want to invest in finding it?"

He wanted it found and the person who took it to be held accountable, period. So I laid out our initial game plan. I told him that we'd start with a Facebook page, a Craig's listing and lots of flyers all around town.

"You think that'll work?"

He forgot what it's like in the small town atmosphere so I had to remind him.

"Hell, yes. This is a tight community and if we put it out there enough I guarantee you someone will have heard something; guaranteed."

He told me who he had purchased the land from and said that he called him as soon as he saw the cabin was missing. He had an agreement with the seller that he could hunt on his land anytime he wanted except during his two weeks. They had this deal in writing and it was for the first five years only, which meant the contract was almost over. The seller told him he was up there a few weekends ago and that the cabin was definitely there that weekend.

He left my office a few hours later more optimistic and encouraged than when he arrived. There really wasn't too much he could do until we got our feelers out there. His yearly trip derailed, he spent the night in a hotel in town and flew home the next day. I promised him we'd keep in touch and I'd let him know when we got a lead.

Kaleb printed close to 100 flyers and distributed them every place he could within 30 miles of where the cabin was taken from. We knew they would grab some attention especially with the heading: "HAVE YOU SEEN THIS CABIN?" It included exterior and interior pictures of the cabin as well as details of where it was stolen from. We said that it was indeed a stolen cabin and ended it with a little incentive that said "compensation for good information can be discussed".

We put that instead of the typical "reward offered" because we learned from that mistake in the past during a case we had regarding a diamond ring. Probably one of our biggest mysteries to date that is still unsolved. It was a typical day at the office and we received a Fed Ex package, nothing unusual, until we opened it. Inside there was a plain white envelope with a balled-up Kleenex in it. On the envelope in black ink was handwritten "Aaron, I know you'll find the rightful owner. Thanks". Whoever sent it knew me enough to know my name but not well enough to know the correct spelling. In the Kleenex was what I'm told by every female I show it to, a gorgeous multi-diamond platinum ring. We had it appraised by a local jeweler and it is worth a pretty penny. No return address or name was on the note. We put an ad in the local newspaper and foolishly put “reward offered”. We had caller after caller saying they were positive it was their ring- not one of those callers could describe it correctly. It’s a unique enough piece of jewelry there’s no faking the description. So our hope is by re-wording the reward sentence only serious leads will come in. There always will be at least a few nut cases.

Kaleb posted the flyers at grocery stores, banks, gas stations, fast food restaurants, post offices, laundry mats and anywhere else they’d let him. It was a crazy amount of posters and he hung each and every one. Then Kaleb started to research hauling companies in the area; calling every company he could find that advertised they moved buildings. He was a few calls in when he came across his first potential lead. Apparently this gentleman used to move buildings, but in the last few years switched over to primarily renting sheds and smaller buildings. He just never changed his advertising. It was when he told Kaleb he had three, not one or two, but three of his buildings stolen. And to add to it he not only knew who did it, but he knew where they were now.

"That's great! Who is it?" Kaleb asked, thinking that the only thing to come out of this guy's mouth was going to be a name, but it wasn't. First, there was an uncomfortable length of silence then a hang up. Kaleb is relentless so he immediately dialed the number and he was a little surprised the man actually answered it. He did apologize for his abrupt action and continued on telling Kaleb this thief was not only a known oxycontin user but was armed to the hilt; he owned a reptile store and was well known in the area as a bully. Fitting really, a snake dealing snakes. This man was terrified of him and this was more than obvious. He described the thief as if he was one of the characters in "Deliverance", and he obviously wanted nothing to do with him. He said that even though he was out over $6,000, he would never risk his family or business over it. He also mentioned he knew who had transported them as well. Kaleb once again pressured him for a name but was met with the same resistance.

"The guy who moved them is a good man and a prominent figure in our town; I'm certain he didn't know they were stolen. I really don't want to get in the middle of this. Sorry."

"If he's a good guy then maybe he can help us right this wrong."

"Well, maybe. But I don't want to be mentioned."

Kaleb assured him that his name wouldn't come up. Who the mover was isn't as shocking as what his job title was. The man who moved this ominous man's sheds was the mayor of the town! In a small town the people that serve the city usually have a regular job as well, and this mayor just so happened to have a business hauling buildings. Could he be the same guy that moved our client's cabin for the Lizard Man? Was there a connection? We had to find this out.

After a bit more research, we found out this guy was a Mennonite. I didn't know this before but apparently this Protestant group of individuals with numerous beliefs do not involve themselves in anything law or legal related. This means they either solve their issues amongst themselves, or they forget them altogether like he had done with his stolen sheds. Still, this was our only real lead so it needed to be pursued.

We decided that Kaleb should take a drive up there and maybe if he met the man face to face he'd be more inclined to share the name of his thief. It was a little after noon when Kaleb got there and it appeared as if the whole town closed up at noon. There was no reaching our lead until after lunch so Kaleb decided he might as well catch a quick bite himself before making a second attempt at his business. There was a limited amount of choices when it came to dining and Kaleb decided to opt for a sit down dinner versus drive thru. He sat down in a fairly crowded café that was filled with what Kaleb assumed were all regulars, which the waitress' opening line confirmed.

"Hi, you're not from around here are you?"

Kaleb, who usually isn't much for chit chat, decided to share why he was in her town. He told her how the owner flew in from Tennessee and found his cabin was stolen right off his land and all that was left was the concrete slab. He then said he was here in town to meet the owner of the place that rented buildings because he knew someone who had stolen from him in the past. Sure that was a slight stretch but it helped his story. He was hopeful that maybe someone had some insight but didn't expect to find out as much as he did from his friendly server.

"I'm so glad Dell finally decided to do something about his sheds. It's about time someone stood up to that creep."

Kaleb acted as if what she told him was old news and continued the conversation hoping to get more information.

"Yeah, I hear he's a bit of a bully. Does he come around here often?"

"Sometimes, his wife comes in more. She's sometimes here in the morning for coffee."

"Oh, but um...um... her husband, sorry I just forgot his name." Kaleb again stretched the truth.

"I don't know his name; we just call him Lizard Man."

"Lizard Man?"

"You know because of their store and all."

Kaleb said nothing and hoped the silence would provoke her to again give a little more information.

"His reptile shop."

Kaleb asked for his food to go and called me the instant he was in his car away from any ears. I was bowled over; could this be our guy or a freak coincidence? The guy who knowingly stole at least three sheds owned a reptile store, and the guy our client bought his land from just so happened to also run a reptile store.

Kaleb decided to visit the snake shop and see if he could maybe get a name and a feel for this character. He walked in to see a rather large man behind the counter with worn-out jeans and a plaid flannel shirt with the sleeves cut off. Now Kaleb is not exactly a small man, so for him to refer to someone as big says a lot. Kaleb did a great job pretending to be in the market for a bearded dragon. I never did ask Kaleb how he knew so much about reptiles and I probably won't. There are certain things I don't need to know. This man told Kaleb that the owner wasn't in so all Kaleb left with was a name on a business card. I was in an appointment so he waited to give me the name until he came back to the office. The minute the name came out of Kaleb's mouth I knew this was our guy! All we needed was the proof.

The next morning I came in to my office at my usual early time. I enjoy coming in before any of the other staff. I get in and start the coffee, and I attempt to catch up on my never-ending emails during the silence. This morning started no differently until the ring of the phone caught me off guard, considering it was way before our typical opening hour. I always assume the type of person who calls when they know the business is closed is either someone selling or someone yelling; one of those automatic telemarketing phone calls or a coward that wants to give you a piece of his mind when he hoped there was no chance of anyone actually answering the phone. Hazard of the job I guess; when you make a living exposing scum there's bound to be some back-lash. I decided to answer it anyway and it was not what I expected.

"Hello. My name is Olivia."

"Hi Olivia, what can I do for you?"

"Are you a private investigator?"

"Yes, what can I help you with?"

I read her silence as hesitation so asked one more time.

"Is there something I can do for you, Olivia?"

"Um, uh. I um, I think I have that cabin you're looking for."

Now it was my turn to be momentarily silent.

"Really?!"

She described it for me with more details than what we had posted on Facebook, Craig's list, or the flyers. It was our cabin all right.

"Oh, that's a bummer."

Probably not what she wanted to hear but we both know what happens to the person who unknowingly buys stolen goods.

"I know. I'm sick to my stomach; I wasn't sure if I even wanted to talk to you."

"Look, Olivia, did you know the cabin was stolen?"

"No! Honestly, I had no idea. I was picking up my mail and saw the flyer posted and I could hardly believe it."

I told her that I believed her and assured her that she wasn't being implicated in the theft. But that didn't exactly comfort her completely.

"Here's my problem. I'm living in it. Am I going to lose my home?"

I didn't have a definite answer for that question but told her I was certain that we could maybe work something out with our client. Again, it didn't completely comfort her.

"Is it possible that there's a dispute over who actually owned it?"

I knew she was grasping but, unfortunately, I did know the answer to this one.

"No, it legally belongs to our client. He has the land deed and the receipts from the cabin and all the work that went into putting it on his property."

"Oh, well it was worth a shot." She murmured.

I then asked her to explain to me how she ended up with this cabin. She started at the very beginning; she saw the ad in the post office, and then she told me of how she went up to the land to see the cabin before actually deciding to buy it. Unbelievable, this guy actually took her onto someone else's property to show the cabin he was about to steal! She said that he had a key to the gate so she didn't think anything of it. Naturally, she fell in love the first time she saw it and said it was perfect for her. She had a small lot outside of the same town where the reptile store was and worried she'd never be able to afford her own place on it, until she saw the cabin advertised. She lived alone with her Jack Russell terrier so the size was ideal. She went to the bank to get a loan and they needed a receipt so he gave her one from his business.

"Do you happen to still have that receipt?" I held my breath knowing this could be the hook we needed.

"Sure, it's with all the bank paperwork. I know that it was an amazing deal and the bank said it was a third of what it's actually worth. But I didn't think anything of that because times are tough, people are giving things away hoping to get ahead. Do you want a copy of it?"

We had him. We had all the proof we needed and he was going down. I just wish I could have given this poor woman the security of knowing that she wasn't going to be homeless. I'm sure my client would work with her, but the bottom line was that she was in the possession of stolen property and if push came to shove, she'd lose. I couldn't wait to make the call to our client, and since he was a few hours ahead of me I made the call as soon as I hung up from her.

Our client was thrilled and confessed that he had doubted we'd be able to help him out. He said it wasn't anything against us, he just knew that this was a challenge most wouldn't have been able to stand up to, let alone complete.

"We can have him in handcuffs before long."

"Do it! This is amazing!"

I told him that we even had his wife as an accessory. According to Olivia, she was with them looking at it on our client's land. I knew he was excited and wanted justice to be served but I also know how our system works, or better yet, doesn't work. So I gave him something else to think about.

"Well, wait a minute. I have another option."

"There's something better than having them behind bars? You haven't disappointed me yet so I'm all ears."

I let him know that the chance of him regaining any of his loss once they're in jail wasn't likely. So I wanted to give him another alternative, one that would at least give him something back.

"Let's add up the total of what you're out. You've got the cabin, the furniture, all other contents that were also stolen, the plane fare here and back, the truck rental, and don't forget my fees."

"Oh and I forgot to mention that when I made the deal four years back I bought three snowmobiles from him that I have yet to see."

"Put them on the list too."

I could hear him on the other end of the phone clicking buttons on a calculator and I gave him time to total everything up.

"Whoa, it's just over $28,000. Well, that doesn't make me feel better."

I don't think he realized his losses were that high. If he wasn't motivated before, he certainly was now.

"Here's what I propose, let me go talk to him. I'll basically lay it on the line and tell him that he's got 48 hours to come up with $28,000 or he's going to jail for felony grand theft."

"Can you do that?? I don't think he has 28 grand."

"That's not our concern. Trust me, if someone came to you and said 'find the cash or go to prison'; you'd find the cash."

"Okay. Let's do that."

I could hear both apprehension and excitement in his voice. Not everyone feels comfortable with confrontation, but for me it's fun, especially with immoral, unethical dirt bags like the Lizard Man.

The next morning, Kaleb and I wired up and decided to take a little road trip with numerous stops on the agenda. Our first visit was to the mayor; if he was indeed innocent then maybe he had some insight for us. We stopped at the City Hall first where his assistant told us that he usually didn't stop in until later in the afternoon on his way home from his day job. Then she gave us his business address as well as his home address, along with the tip that he goes home for lunch. It was already half past twelve so we decided to mosey on over to his house.

We saw his truck in the driveway and as we strolled up the walkway, we heard voices behind the front door.

"Bam, bam, bam." Then silence. What? I looked at Kaleb and just shook my head.

"Bam, bam, bam." This time I intentionally knocked a lot louder, enough that it got their dog's attention and he was barking right behind the door. But still nothing from the people.

"Bam, bam, bam." Last attempt. We heard footsteps come towards us but then the only thing that happened was that the dog was muffled. Really? This is a mind changer; I no longer think our mayor is as innocent as we were originally told.

We left and parked the car down the block, far enough not to be seen but could still see the house. Less than 15 minutes after we left someone opened the front door and let the little barker out to do his business. Okay, fine, we can play that way.

We went back to City Hall and once again chatted with the mayor's assistant. I gave her my card and told her to tell her boss to call me the minute he came in. I also told her to inform him that I knew he was home. She looked at me confused but her boss wouldn't be. Our next stop was to the mayor's day job and what we found next did not help his cause at all. He was in business with a local log home builder and when we saw the name on the building we both froze. His partner just so happened to have the same last name as Lizard Man! The mayor was partners with the dad; the father built them and the mayor moved them. I was now fairly convinced that the mayor knew what he was into, especially after our little game of hide-and-seek. Something stinks! Our next stop was Lizard's house.

We pulled up and immediately saw a woman outside. She watched us get out of the car and like most of us would do, she waited to see what we needed.

"Hi, is your husband home?"

"No, he should be at work."

"Are you his wife?" She nodded.

"Can I help you with something?"

I handed her my card and waited to read her reaction; her eyes got wide and she froze just for a split second.

"I need to talk to your husband about the cabin he stole."

I didn't think it was possible but her eyes got even wider and I swear I saw her knees buckle slightly.

"You'll have to talk to my husband. I don't know anything about a cabin."

"Yeah, you do. You were there showing the cabin to Olivia, you know, the woman that bought it? I have him on three felonies: criminal trespassing, burglary and grand theft. You're an accessory to all of them. Oh, and I'm working on an additional felony charge with the Feds for money laundering since you funneled the money through your business."

Kaleb and I watched her and weren't sure if she was going to pee her pants or pass out. She got the message loud and clear. We left her and told her to tell her hubby to call me by noon the next day or they'd be in handcuffs soon. I would bet everything I own that she was on the phone with her husband before she took her next breath.

I barely had a chance to sit down when we returned to the office and the phone rang; it was Mr. Mayor.

"Are you aware that the cabin you moved for your partner's son was stolen?" I asked.

There's nothing like a person's first reaction for me to know what the truth is and what it is not. If someone just told you that you had something to do with stolen merchandise and you're innocent, you're initial reaction is one of shock, or denial at best. The mayor's reaction told me all I needed to know. His response was silence, followed by awkward stuttering. It was obvious I had caught him off guard and that he didn't have time to prepare a lie; his voice was nervous and his thoughts were random. He never admitted guilt but he didn't have to. I asked him who helped him and he willingly gave me the number of one of his employees. I think he thought that if he appeared helpful he'd look less guilty; he was wrong. I then spoke with this employee who did have the reaction I expected from an innocent man. He gave me a list of all the buildings he moved for the mayor in the last few months. All of three buildings were also stolen – big surprise.... This story kept getting better and better.

Later that day my phone buzzed and I received a text; a text from Lizard Man. It was long and random. He started out apologizing for not being able to call because he was in a meeting, and how this was all a big misunderstanding and that nothing was illegal. He went on repeating the same thing over again and then he hung himself. He volunteered to build our client a new cabin exactly like the one that "went missing" on the exact same spot. He then typed that he knew a guy who would even do the electrical for him. He ended by saying that he'll try and call me after the meeting.

Bull! So I dialed him immediately. His wife answered and told me that he was in a meeting. They weren't the smartest crooks because if he truly was in a meeting, the phone he just texted me from should have been in there with him! Duh. She didn't appreciate me bringing this fact to her attention, and decided to respond in anger and started yelling into the speaker.

"You've got nothing! How dare you do this to us?"

Yeah, I don't need this crap so I loudly cut her off mid-stream.

"Stop!" She did so and I made my final point. "I guess you've decided not to cooperate, that's fine, and it's your decision. The sheriff's department will be in touch you both soon."

Click.

My next call was to our client with a step-by-step account of events, including the call I just hung up on, and he had the same response I did.

"Let's nail them!"

I immediately turned everything over to the Sheriff's department. And *somehow*, *someone* talked to the local newspapers and the entire case went public the next day. Wonder how that happened? ☺

Here's what we know:

- Lizard Man stole our client's cabin and its contents.

- The town's mayor moved a stolen cabin. Whether he knew it was stolen or not, we will let you decide.

- Our client agreed to let Olivia live in the cabin until the following spring. He is a nice guy!

The Rule: If your house/cabin has been stolen go to the local reptile shop and ask for it back. The guy and his wife that own the store are not the sharpest knives in the drawer.

Unfortunately, what we don't know are the consequences of Mr. and Mrs. Lizard Man as the charges were still pending when this book was printed.

Check out our website for results, and be certain to read the finale in the next book of "The Rules" Series.

BUT WAIT…THERE'S MORE!

Thank you for buying our book, and contributing to my ultimate goal of retiring on a golf course.

If you happened to borrow it from a friend, thanks for reading it. But if you're a true friend you'll jump off your wallet and buy the next in the series and then let your buddy read it.

We've had a ton of *crazy* cases and have only begun to share them with you! Look for these titles in the near future:

- RULES OF SERVES & SUBPOENAS
- RULES OF CHILD CUSTODY & DIVORCE CASES
- RULES OF RUNAWAYS
- RULES OF WORKER'S COMP FRAUD
- RULES OF SURVEILLANCE
- RULES OF MISSING PERSONS
- RULES OF WACKO's (Cases NOT to Take)

The next in line, which can be yours by sacrificing only two or three morning lattes, will not disappoint you. And it is the:

RULES OF MISSING PERSONS

One case we will be telling you is about Henry Long. Henry was an alcoholic transit who disappeared at age 20. His parents, who were now in their eighties, had not heard from him in over twenty five years. They had hired PI after PI to find him and spent thousands of dollars trying to find out anything about his whereabouts; to no avail. They called me just to see if I could recommend a PI in the Seattle area (his last known address) that they could hire to find him. I went to their home to meet with them and I took the case. The following two months were a real adventure!

Any opinions expressed in The Private Dick Diaries are solely those of the author. Any quotes, theories or references from any source, being private or public, are not intended to convey this author's opinion. Some cases and anecdotes are from public records and from many different jurisdictions of several states. Names and descriptions of places and facts have been fictionalized and disguised to protect the identities of all persons involved.

Second Edition: October 11, 2012

Visit our websites:

www.theprivatedickdiaries.com

www.idahoprivateeye.com

Published by: The Private Dick Diaries, LLC

Printed in the USA

Tales from Erin Jenkins – Private Investigator

Written by CJ Vertefeuille